Tales of Old Norfolk

This book is to be returned on or before
the last date stamped below.

Other counties in this series include:

Tales of
Old Norfolk

Polly Howat

With illustrations by Don Osmond

COUNTRYSIDE BOOKS
NEWBURY, BERKSHIRE

First Published 1991
© Polly Howat 1991
Reprinted 1993

COUNTRYSIDE BOOKS
3 CATHERINE ROAD
NEWBURY, BERKSHIRE

ISBN 1 85306 129 8

Designed by Mon Mohan
Produced through MRM Associates Ltd., Reading
Typeset by Wessex Press Design & Print Ltd., Warminster
Printed in England

For Gordon and Myra Scivier

Acknowledgements

With thanks to the Directors of Norfolk Lavender Ltd for their generous access to archive material.

Also to Ernest and Jean Cole, Stan Webster, Charles Lewis, Curator of the Maritime Museum, Great Yarmouth, and the many other people who have contributed towards the writing of this book.

Contents

CONTENTS

NORFOLK – The map overleaf is by John Speede, and shows the county as it was in the early seventeenth century.

NORFOL

A COVNTI

FLORISHIN

& POPVLO

DESCRIBE

AND DEVID

DIEV ET MON DROIT

With twoe feverall and vnnaturall rebellions hath this Countie
of Norfolk bene infested: the first commenced by Iohn Litster a
Dyer in Norwich calling himselfe kinge of the Commons whoe
led fyftye thousand Souldiers into the feild and forceibly caryed
the Lord Morley and Scales to serve him at his table with other
Esquiles besides but was lastly overthrown by Henry Spencer bishop
of Norwich and worthely hanged. Iune. 1582.
The other was vnder the leading of Robert Kit Tannar of
Windham whoe in a conflict forced the Lord William Parre
Marquess of Northampton to flight: and slewe the Lord Shef-
feild in the feild but after many outrages done to the citie
of Norwich was taken by Iohn Dudley Earle of Warwick having fyve thousand of his folowers slaine and himself hanged vpm the tope of the Castle. Ano. 1549.

THE WASHE

WEST

MERSHE
LANDE

FREBRIDGE IN MERSHLAND
HVNDRED

PARTE OF

CAMBRIDGE

SHIRE

ELY

SMITHDON
HVN

GRENEHAWE
HVN: Felde Dowli
HVN:

BROTHER
CROS

GALLOWE

LAVNDICHE
HVN:

FREBRIDGE
Citra LINN

HVN:

CLACKHOWSE

S GRENEHOWE

WAYLAND
HVN:

HVN:

HVN:

GRIMSHOO HVNDRED

LACKFORD
HVN:

Thetforde

Described by Christopher Saxton augmen
ted by I. Speede. In to behold in popes
head Illey by I. S. & G. H. cum privil.

A Sc

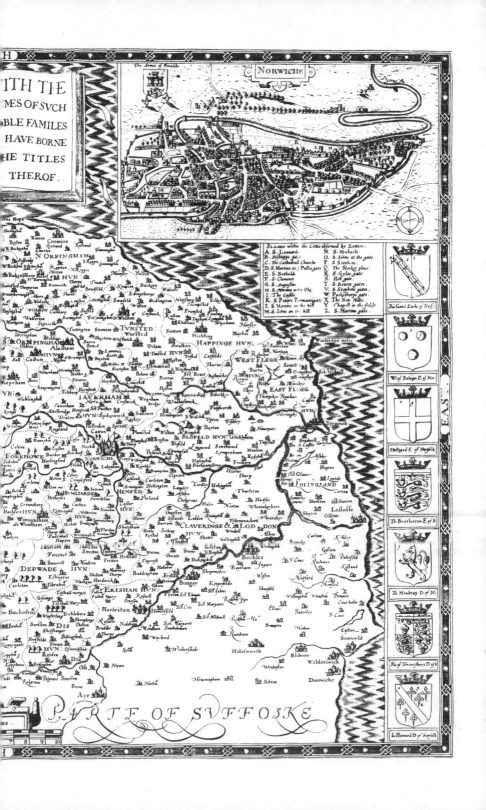

Will Kemp
and his
'Nine Daies Wonder'

IT was during Lent in 1599 that an enormous and excited crowd gathered in Norwich. The streets were buzzing with the anticipated merriment of seeing Master Will Kemp, the celebrated and flamboyant Elizabethan dancer and actor, who had danced with a jingle and jangle of bells around his ankles, every inch from London to Norwich in just nine days. He actually arrived in the city just over three weeks from his leaving the capital, the extra time being taken up with periods of rest.

Will Kemp is mentioned in several of Shakespeare's plays by name and it has been suggested that the parts of Dogberry in *Much Ado About Nothing* and Peter in *Romeo and Juliet* were written specially to suit his qualities. Several contemporary composers dedicated dance tunes to this energetic young man.

Being short of money at that time he undertook this great dance both to raise funds and promote himself. He obtained private sponsorship and collected money en route. In return he took a quantity of gaily coloured garters which he gave to anyone who took his fancy or helped him in any way.

Eventually the story of his journey, which was often quite distorted, became the subject of many tavern songs and ballads. This angered Will Kemp who was compelled to write his own version of his *'Nine Daies' Wonder performed in a daunce from London to Norwich'*. He dedicated the tale to Mistress Anne Fitton, a maid of honour to Queen Elizabeth.

He left the City just before 7.00 am on the first Monday of Lent accompanied by Thomas Slye, piper and taborer, William Bee, his servant and George Spratt, umpire and timekeeper. An illustration which appeared in his *Nine Daies Wonder* published in 1600 shows him dressed as a Morris dancer.

A great crowd accompanied the sparkling trio to the outskirts of London, offering them food and drink which Kemp refused to take in any quantity for fear of overstuffing himself. All along his route little entertainments were arranged to amuse his followers. It was late on the first night that he finally reached Romford where he accepted a lift on horseback to his lodgings. They stayed in this town for two days after which time he was taken to the place where he had stopped dancing and from where he resumed his energetic travels.

He hopped and skipped to the jolly music coming from Thomas Slye's pipe which he played with one hand, the other beating a rhythm on his small drum which would have hung from a cord from his waist or neck.

At times he was almost knocked over by the crowds as they jostled about him. Another danger was the mud-rucked cart tracks which threatened to break or sprain his ankles. Sometimes people would dance alongside him, but could not match his pace and soon gave up with a stitch in their sides and gasping for breath.

Gallant Will danced through Essex and into Suffolk, by which time snow was falling heavily and he was forced to stop at one resting place for six nights, which was probably a welcome break. Greatly restored he danced ten miles into Norfolk in less than three hours. He wrote about this achievement that he 'far'd like one that had escaped the stockes and tride the use of his legs to outrun the Constable'. In Thetford it was the time of the Assizes and an even greater crowd received him. Kemp was entertained for the weekend by Sir Edwin Rich who gave him £5.

Considerably richer and much rested he danced off on the Monday morning bound for Rockland where he was booked in for the night at an inn. The landlord greeted him decked out in his best clothes and clutching a well prepared speech but he was so confused by the grandness of the occasion that he began his welcome as, 'O Kemp, Deere Master Kemp, you are even as welcome as . . .' He lost his words and in an embarrassed manner stuttered, 'as the Queen's best greyhound'.

Kemp breakfasted well and hopped and jingled to Hingham, pushing the jubilant crowd from his path. The following day which was Wednesday took him towards his finishing post. His approach to Norwich was clogged with people and he was begged to delay his entrance to the city until the authorities could control the crowd. The city dignitaries had positioned their families at the best vantage points whilst around them seethed a huge tangle of old people and young, rich and poor, bawling babes and barking dogs, hawkers and traders, all come to cheer the famous Morris dancer from London.

Dancing was halted just outside St Giles' Gate and the hero was brought on horseback to be presented to the mayor and his aldermen. They welcomed him most cordially and agreed to meet all his expenses.

On the following Saturday he was taken to St Giles' Gate where he had finished his dancing three days earlier and resumed his task, entering the city this time at St Stephen's. The wifflers (men appointed to clear the way during processions and ceremonies) had a hard task keeping order and holding back the crowds who by this time were almost hysterical. Thomas Gilbert read the official address and the City Waits were gathered at the Market Cross to welcome him with songs.

Kemp writes, 'such Waytes (under Benedicite let it be spoken) few Citties in our Realme have the like, none better; who, besides their excellency in wind instruments, their rare cunning on the Vyoll and the Violin, they'r voices be admirable, everie one of the(m) able to serve in any Cathedrale Church in Christendoome for Quiristers.'

It was difficult for the trio to wend their way through the narrow streets and on one occasion Will collided with a buxom girl. He caught his foot in her skirt, which was ripped from her waist to the ground, much to the delight of the onlookers who cheered and cat-called, turning the poor girl's face an even deeper shade of red. Will threw her a garter and proceeded with the last leg of his journey.

In best showman fashion he took a mighty leap over the churchyard wall at St John's, thus shortening his distance to the mayor's house, who at that time was Roger Weild, a wealthy merchant who lived in a simple fashion but treated the dancer well. Kemp wrote that his example of modesty could well be followed by other less praiseworthy businessmen. Roger Weild donated £5 in Elizabethan angels to Kemp's well filled purse. The angel was a gold coin bearing the figure of the archangel Michael slaying the dragon. The mayor also granted him 40 shillings a year for life which would help to keep the debtors away.

At the end of his story Kemp condemns those who accused him of making a great fortune from his stunt. He explained that after all expenses had been deducted he had only made a modest profit which was a fair reward for his labours. Many of his sponsors had failed to meet their debt and he had deposited sums of money with each, to be repaid in triplicate at the end of his successful journey. He threatened to publish the names of all those who had offered him money, marking against each either the letter 'H' for honest or 'before the other Bench-Whistlers shall stand "K" for ketlers (knaves) or Keistrels.'

He concludes by threatening 'the impudent generation of Balladmongers and their coherents' that if they wrote any more false accounts of his travels and invented other journeys for him he would take 'terrible vengeance' on them all.

Kemp's life following his trip to Norwich is vague. He acted for a time with the Earl of Worcester's company of players and there are tales that he went Morris dancing through Germany to Rome and even crossed the Alps to the tune of the fife and drum, but with regard to the latter nothing has been substantiated.

The Tabernacle Street Murder

As the bells were ringing in the New Year of 1869 a short, elderly, well dressed man presented himself at Carter Street police station in Walworth, South London. He was William Sheward from Norwich and he confessed to such a diabolical crime that Inspector James Davis thought the little man must be either drunk or mad.

Sheward subsequently dictated his statement which began, 'I William Sheward of Norwich, charge myself with the wilful murder of my wife.' It had happened almost 18 years previously at their home at 7, Tabernacle Street (now Bishopgate) Norwich on 14th June, 1849.

The report of his terrible crime was to cause a thrill of horror from one end of England to another, it having all the ingredients which sold popular newspapers: cold-blooded murder, sex, butchery, bankruptcy, and finally capital punishment.

They married in London in 1836 when William was 24 years old and worked as a pawnbroker's assistant. His bride, Martha Francis, born at Wymondham, Norfolk, and 14 years his senior, worked as a domestic servant.

Soon after their marriage they moved to Wymondham where they lodged with Martha's twin sister, Mary Bunn. They later moved to Norwich where there were better employment prospects for William, who resumed his old occupation as a tailor. Their marriage was not particularly happy and in time William had various love affairs with younger women. He moved from employer to employer and eventually started his own tailoring

15

businesses which soon flopped. In 1849 he was declared bankrupt and the Shewards' marriage was on the rocks. Sheward went to work for Mr Christie, a Norwich pawnbroker with whom he deposited £400, presumably to keep it from the hands of his creditors, which greatly annoyed Martha.

The couple were constantly rowing about money and on Saturday 14th June, 1851 after a particularly bad altercation Sheward said that he grabbed a razor and slashed her throat. Her blood spurted everywhere and William had to bath himself before setting off to keep an appointment at Great Yarmouth. Martha lay where she had fallen, to await Sheward's attention later.

By day he continued to work as a pawnbroker's assistant, but at night he turned into a fiendish butcher, hacking and sawing in a terrible and urgent fashion.

The weather was hot and Sheward admitted that the house soon started to smell. Each night he had to light a fire in his room to mask the stench before starting work. He first boiled Martha's head, hands and feet, which he then chopped up into little pieces. The rest of her body was given the same treatment, but without cooking. Her remains were then put into a pail and distributed around Norwich. Martha's entrails were stuffed down a drain. On the Sunday following the murder the house was cleaned from top to bottom and all the bloodstained items were burned.

Although bits of the body had been discovered just one week after their secretion, no-one linked Mrs Sheward's disappearance with the grisly finds. Sheward said that his wife had gone to New Zealand to find a former lover and his plausible story was believed, for Martha had quite a chequered past. They had few friends and little contact with their relations. Three months later he moved from Tabernacle Street and rented three rooms in King Street. He continued to work for Mr Christie, who suspected nothing.

The years passed and Sheward had plenty of girl friends. He was a heavy drinker and spent much of his time in the local taverns. Eventually he lived for nine years with Charlotte Buck with whom he had three children. On 13th February 1862 they were married at Norwich registry office, Charlotte knowing nothing about his past life.

His second marriage appears to have been a watershed for soon he spent even more time drinking and the alcohol made him talk in his sleep. He aged prematurely and became consumed with guilt over his long ago crime. He left Christie's employ and started his own pawnbroking business without success. He then became the landlord of the Key and Castle inn in Oak Street, where he lived with his wife and children. By now his guilt was driving him to the edge of madness.

Possibly the Christmas festivities of 1868 brought matters to a head, for on Tuesday 29th December he bid his family and customers goodbye and, armed with a razor, caught the train to London determined to commit suicide. For two days he wandered around London, trying to summon up enough courage to kill himself. Then on New Year's Eve he visited the house in Walworth where he had first met his wife, Martha. The memories and guilt provoked by this visit made Sheward give himself up to the law. He decided to unburden himself at Carter Street police station.

Sheward was taken back to Norwich where it was confirmed that pieces of a human body had been found in the city at the time of the alleged crime. After five appearances before the Magistrates he was committed to the Norwich Spring Assizes and stood trial on 29th March, 1869. The public pushed and shoved each other in the hope of gaining admittance to the hearing. The successful ones witnessed the pathetic sight of the diminutive William Sheward who was carried into the dock by two warders. He could not walk because of the rheumatism which he suffered in both ankles and his frailty was out of keeping with the popular image of a person who could kill and hack his wife to pieces, no matter when the crime had taken place.

The hearing lasted two days, and much of the evidence caused many of the women in the court to feel faint and nauseated.

It was Charles Johnson's dog finding the hand in a wood one week after the alleged crime which had alerted the authorities to the foul deed, which had never been linked to the disappearance of Martha Sheward. Harry Layton had found a foot lying in a churchyard. Charlie Sales had been a sewerman in 1851 and had recovered the entrails and other parts from a drain close to the Sheward's home. The ladies gulped and reached for their smelling salts.

Martha's family testified that Sheward had told them she had gone to New Zealand to search out a former lover, a carpenter named Worseldine. They said their brother-in-law had pointed out that if his errant wife wished to contact them she would do so. He had no idea of her whereabouts and they had believed him.

It took the jury just one and a quarter hours to reach their verdict, which was Guilty. The prisoner in the dock remained impassive as the death sentence was pronounced. He execution was fixed for Monday 19th April, 1869 but the executioner had a prior appointment with death at Gloucester Prison, so the 'Norfolk Butcher' had to wait until the following day.

Public hangings had recently been abolished so he was executed in the privacy of Norwich gaol. Sheward had to be carried to the gallows because of his rheumatism, and the prison bell tolled mournfully. Perhaps in his tormented mind the authorities were about to perform that which he had been too scared to undertake?

A black flag was hoisted over the prison gate which signalled to the large crowd outside that Calcroft the executioner had accomplished his task.

The Eccentric
Dr Messenger Monsey

BORN in 1693, the son of the Reverend Robert Monsey, Messenger Monsey lived at Whitwell, Norfolk, for most of his young years. He earned a place amongst Norfolk's 'Worthies' from his strange appearance and razor sharp tongue. His unusual christian name was in memory of August Messenger, from whom his father inherited the large Whitwell estate soon after losing his living at Bawdeswell for refusing to take the oaths of allegiance to William III after the Glorious Revolution of 1688.

Young Monsey graduated from Cambridge in 1711 and eventually practised medicine at Bury St Edmund's where he settled down with his wife and only child Charlotte to enjoy the comfortable routine of a country doctor. Yet he hardly looked the part dressed 'with a rusty wig, dirty boots and leather breeches, with the commonplace questions learned by rote, the tongue, the pulse and the guinea.'

His entire life was changed on the day that the second Earl of Godolphin was taken ill at Newmarket. Monsey was sent to attend the earl, who made a complete recovery and a life-long friendship was forged between the two men, each having a similar disposition.

After his wife's death Monsey moved to London, leaving his child in the care of relatives. Lord Godolphin became his patron and offered up his home at St James to be shared with his friend. Employment was found as a non-resident physician at Chelsea Hospital.

He was soon absorbed into his patron's circle of friends who, although not particularly liking the man, were enthralled by his bad dress sense, terrible table manners and acerbic wit. Life was never dull when Messenger Monsey was about. He became friends with Sir Robert Walpole, the first English Prime Minister and a fellow Norfolk man. Monsey was said to be the only person allowed to contradict the statesman and score over him at billiards.

The scruffy little man was never short of a meal, his presence being continuously sought at dinner parties which he livened up with his sense of fun and lively conversation. His favourite sport was to verbally attack the actor Garrick whose social climbing became the prime target of Monsey's viperous tongue.

One night whilst dining at the Garricks' home in company with some especially valued friends, Monsey grew exasperated with Mrs Garrick who for some reason was serving the food, and taking a long time over the task. Bursting with rage he bawled down the table to her, 'You little confounded toad, will you or will you not send me a wing, leg, bit of breast, rump or merry-thought of one of those chickens?'

Another target for attack was his foresworn adversary Samuel Johnson, the poet, critic and lexicographer whom he enjoyed scandalising in front of a good audience.

Monsey was suspicious of bankers and never used their services. During the summer months he hid his money under a neatly laid fire in his sitting room. His assets tumbled on the day his housekeeper lit a surprise fire on an unseasonally cold day.

He was a good physician but had a strange way of pulling his own teeth. For probably hundreds of years, and certainly within living memory, people without access to proper medical treatment have drawn their own teeth and those of their family with pliers kept especially for this purpose or secured a piece of string around the offending tooth, tied the other end to a door handle and then got someone to slam the door shut.

It is not known why a doctor should want to perform such an operation when he had plenty of medical colleagues, but this was his choice and provided entertainment for his friends. Eschewing the above methods he always favoured a gun. One end of fine cord was tied to his tooth and the other tightly around a bullet which was fired from the firearm. The tooth flew from his gum like a cork from a champagne bottle.

Concerning religion, he professed his belief in the Deity but shocked orthodox Christians by his disbelief in the Holy Trinity, saying it was tantamount to worshipping three Gods. He denounced the Athanasian Creed which he regarded as 'nonsense' and left money in his will to two clergymen who had left the Church as they too could no longer accept the Creed.

When it came to politics he felt that Great Britain was on the brink of impending ruin and in 1779 said that 'French or no French, America or no America, we are undone, and that you and I may easily see without spectacles'. He went on to say it was fine to trust in Providence, 'but let us never hope that He will interfere in preserving a set of such infamous blackguard riotous impious dissolute luxurious Scoundrels as we are from top to bottom.'

None of his other patrons were keen to offer him quarters following the death of Lord Godolphin in 1766. He was therefore obliged to find residence at the Chelsea Hospital, which he loathed as much as his colleagues loathed him.

His declining years were lonely. Charlotte was married to a linen-draper in the City and too busy rearing a large family to bother much about her eccentric father. Until prevented through blindness he took to writing long rambling and overheated letters in spidery handwriting to his family and friends outside the capital. Large portions were devoted to religion, politics, scandal-mongering and his own mortality.

He died on Boxing Day, 1788 aged 95, leaving a will typical of his personality by stipulating that his body should be dissected by either Foster or Cruickshank, London surgeons, to 'find out the matter with my heart, arteries and kidneys. The remainder of my carcass may be put into a hole or crammed into a box with holes and thrown into the Thames, at the pleasure of the surgeon.' Mr Foster carried out the dissection and lectured on the result. He also made a drawing of Messenger Monsey, deceased, from which he commissioned a professional portrait.

After awarding several strange legacies he left word to a certain young woman that he would have left her a sizeable gift if he had not discovered her to be 'a pert conceited minx with as many affected silly airs as a foolish woman of quality.'

THE ECCENTRIC DR MESSENGER MONSEY

He wrote his own epitaph which ended:

'What the next world may be, never troubled my pate:
If not better than this, I beseech thee, oh Fate,
When the bodies of millions fly up in a riot
To let the old carcass of Monsey lie quiet.'

King John's Disaster

Have you heard the schoolboy joke about King John? Question: Why didn't he wear a crown? Answer: Because he lost it in the Wash!

The loss of King John's baggage train in the Wash has become one of an assorted collection of pieces of popular history known to many people. There is no proof that he lost his crown jewels in the terrible disaster of 1216, but it is thought that his baggage train and a huge number of lives were lost in quicksand somewhere between the Walpoles in Norfolk and Sutton Bridge, Lincolnshire. There are many theories and much speculation woven into this tale.

King John, who was crowned in May 1199, was not a popular king. His disastrous foreign policy and arbitrary government soon alienated the goodwill of the English nobility.

According to Matthew Paris, a chronicler of that time, 'On St Edmund's Day, November 20th, 1214, the earls and barons of England met at St Edmund's Bury (Suffolk). . . . The Primate of All England stood at the high end of the altar, and thither advanced each peer according to seniority, and laying his hand on the altar, swore solemnly that if the King would not consent to acknowledge the rights which they claimed, they would withdraw their fealty and make war upon him, till by a charter under his own seal he should confirm their just demands.'

This action finally resulted in the signing of the Magna Carta, at Runnymede, on 19th June, 1215, which defined the barons' feudal obligations to the monarch, opposed his arbitrary application of justice and confirmed the liberties of the English

Church. However this was annulled by the pope and reissued with some changes in 1216, 1217 and 1225.

It was soon evident that the King was waiting for an opportunity for revenge on the triumphant barons and it was not long after the signing that John began to employ mercenaries from the continent and to provision and garrison his castles. He advanced to St Albans, where he divided his army into two parts. One section was ordered to devastate Middlesex, Essex and the adjoining counties, while he himself advanced to Nottingham, burning en route the residences of the barons and plundering their estates.

In the year 1216 the war was at its greatest height and the King was ravaging Norfolk. King's Lynn (then Lynn or Bishop's Lynn) was generally sympathetic to John, who assembled his troops there between 9th and 11th October of that year. During his stay, on the petition of John de Grey, Bishop of Norwich, he granted the town a charter to be a free borough for ever, and other privileges. At the same time the King presented to the Corporation a large, elegant loving-cup and gave them his personal sword.

He left Lynn with his army and large baggage train on 11th October, 1216. There are two schools of thought; one says he was heading straight north, the other that he was first visiting Wisbech. The former believe that it was the tragedy which forced him to make the detour to Wisbech, being the nearest seaport town, to arrange for his salvaged goods to be shipped to the north. Others say he became detached from his column, having eaten a surfeit of lampreys at Wisbech Castle, being taken ill and forced to spend the night there. His army marched on ahead of their monarch.

The venue of the accident also comes into dispute. Was it the Walpole Island area between the Walpoles and Sutton Bridge or was it in the Wellstream, close to Wisbech and Walsoken, Norfolk? In the 13th century the Wellstream ran north through Wisbech and carried all the major water of Fenland, except the Welland and part of the Nene, the latter draining into the Wellstream at Tydd Gote.

The popular account of that fateful journey relates how the King's troops went ahead of the King, who was reacting badly to his big dish of lampreys, and marched to the North to quell the rebels, travelling via Swineshead, Lincolnshire. They crossed the Wash and came to grief in the Walpole Island area, having misjudged the tide and were all swallowed up in the quicksand.

Between 1225–1230 the chronicler Roger Wendover, who was said to specialise in the sensational, wrote an account of the tragic events. The King 'lost all his waggons, carts and packhorses, with his treasures and precious vessels, and everything which he loved with special care.' 'The ground opened in the midst of the waves, and there were bottomless whirl-pools which engulfed everything, with men and horses, so that no man escaped to tell the King of the disaster.'

Matthew Paris also wrote about the King's loss which included, 'his carts, his packhorses, with loot and booty, and all his treasures and household goods', the quicksand 'swallowing up men, arms, tents, victuals and all the King's valuable possessions except his life.' His last remark perhaps leads us to believe that the King was with his men.

There is no proof that the King was carrying his regalia, but he was carrying a lot of coinage with which to pay his men garrisoned in his castles. To account for the loss of the former, for the crown jewels were never seen again, it has been suggested that during the civil war the King had borrowed a considerable sum of money from Bordeaux and Ghent and the regalia may have been used as security. There is also another possibility, put forward by Mr J. C. Holt during his lecture to the friends of the Wisbech and Fenland Museum. King John died at Newark, Lincolnshire, during the night of the 18th. Once dead he was robbed like his father before him, by the members of his household, who looted his goods. 'It is possible that, as unwitting accessories, they [the 13th century chroniclers] have foisted on later generations a tale of treasure first conceived by the jackals who surrounded John's bed as he lay dying at Newark Castle.'

Returning to the awful joke — is there any substance in it? We are told that only a plain golden band was placed on the head of Henry III when he succeeded his father in 1216, but whether this was due to the quicksand, debtors or robbers, we shall never know. Treasure hunters still try their luck around the reputed areas of the accident, but nothing has been discovered.

Food and Drink
from 'Dumplingshire'

NORFOLK was once famous for its dumplings, made from flour, yeast, water and a pinch of salt, and kneaded as only a Norfolk woman knew how. When of the right consistency they were put in boiling liquid for exactly 20 minutes — hence their name — 'Twenty Minute Swimmers'. They were proclaimed fit for a king or a ploughman from 'Dumplingshire'.

Until recent times many families relied upon suet crust to fill their impoverished and empty stomachs and some old people still eat a suet roll, often filled with onions, before their main dinner, a throwback to the times when meat was a luxury. It was always 'father and the boys' who got the lion's share of the meat, 'mother and the girls' came last.

Even the Christmas pudding was cooked in a casing made from a stiff dough. When cold the pastry was chipped off and kept the children quiet for a long time as they gnawed away at the spicy sweetness.

Local wives took great pride in their fluffy 'Norfolk Apple Dumplings', which were whole, cored apples, filled with sugar and sometimes a little spice, then carefully wrapped in a suet crust and baked in the oven. George III is said to have asked a very puzzling question when he was tucking into his apple dumpling. However did the apple get there in the first place? His host is then supposed to have told him the 'Legend of the First Apple Dumpling'.

There was once a Norfolk farmer who had a pretty young wife with rosy cheeks. He loved her complexion which he said

reminded him of ripe apples. She looked so good that he could eat her.

'So you shall', replied his wife in a teasing way, 'but you shall have to wait until tomorrow!' The next dinnertime she set before him what was to become the father of all apple dumplings, soft and succulent inside and gently crisp on the outside. The delighted farmer ate the dumpling, gave his wife a big kiss and money to buy some coloured ribbons at the next fair. The clever girl had instinctively known the way to a Norfolkman's heart.

Another once popular and inexpensive county delicacy, again using apples, was 'Norfolk Biffins'. Like the complexion of the farmer's wife, biffins are red-cheeked apples and were especially popular in Norwich. The apples were dried out very slowly for about five hours encased in clean straw over a wire rack in a barely warm oven. When ready they were taken out and pressed to flatten them without breaking their skins, returned to the oven for an hour and then pressed again. When cold they were rubbed with clarified sugar.

The grand time for feasting was at pig-killing time, when numbers of strange dishes were concocted from every bit of the animal. Chitterling (intestines) and apple pie made a rare dish. The adults and children enjoyed the 'scraps' which were made from all the tiny pieces of saved fat, which were fried until most of the grease had run out. 'When of a delicate brown, they are eaten with a little salt, and much gusto, to the wonder of the town looker-on, who sits by wondering how the eaters can keep them down.' You can now buy these 'Pork Scratchings' in packets, but they are not like mother made.

For people on a low wage, meat still is a luxury. In the old days meat meals generally meant pig. If there was room it was reared for the table in a sty at the bottom of the garden. Its diet was mainly scraps from the table boiled up with small or old potatoes. The animal was not fussy, it would eat and drink almost anything, neither were cold and hungry humans who often got to the hot pig swill before the porker and stole a morsel of potato.

There is an old country saying that the best picture you can have on your wall is a flitch of bacon. It was traditional in some close-knit communities for neighbours to give each other a piece of meat or a string of sausages at the time of their own pig's slaughter, the gift being repaid when his pig was butchered. Sometimes debts owed to local tradesmen were paid off in pig meat.

The words 'Norfolk' and 'Turkey' go together as deliciously as 'Sage' and 'Onion'. The traditional black plumed Norfolk turkeys were introduced to England shortly after 1540. Merchants first introduced them to Greece, then part of the Turkish Empire. The Greeks called them Turkeys because they looked so like their pompous Turkish masters, the red head-piece looking like a fez.

Until quite recently parts of the county were over-run with rabbits, which offered a plentiful supply of meat to poor people, especially those living in the sandy soil areas. Known as 'hollow-meat', they were fed a lot to farm servants and, as their counterparts from Scotland were said to have stipulated against salmon, so it was the practice here that when a servant let himself to a farmer he made provision that he should eat 'hollow-meat' only on a certain number of days a week.

There was plenty of free food to be obtained from the country, legally or otherwise. A lady from Marshland St James, near Wisbech, remembers that when times were hard she and her brothers were sent out at night with lanterns to dazzle blackbirds roosting in the hedgerows. The birds were plucked and cleaned, their legs, wings and heads removed and their bodies baked in a pie. She said that sparrows made good eating and children loved to trap them under a potato riddle (sieve) which was jacked up on one end with a stick to which was tied a long piece of string. Grains of corn were put under the riddle, you waited patiently at a distance and when there were a few birds happily pecking away at the grain the string was given a tug, away fell the stick and down came the sieve. In time there were enough birds to cook in the same fashion as the blackbirds.

Killing swans is now illegal but they too were once a great delicacy and readily available from Norfolk's wet regions.

Within memory certain days were celebrated with particular dishes which were great treats for low paid families and especially welcomed by their children. Easter Sunday saw Tansy Pudding on the dishes of many Norfolk families, a delicious concoction of almonds, tansy juice, cream and eggs. Cheese cakes and baked custards were treats for Whitsuntide and goose at Michaelmas.

Goosegrease was saved for rubbing over chests to stop winter coughs and colds.

Many housewifes baked a small loaf or 'cake' of bread each Good Friday. It was the same recipe as usual but especially well baked and stored carefully until the following Good Friday. Bread baked on this day was said to never go mouldy. Sometimes small pieces were broken off and mixed with water to cure diarrhoea, for which it was considered a 'sovereign remedy'. The last crumbs of the old bread were eaten on the anniversary of its baking to ensure good luck through the ensuing year.

Mead was a popular drink into this century and was made by beekeepers. It was very sweet, and very strong. Made from water, honey and egg whites, it was spiced with cinnamon, mace, ginger and cloves. When fermentation had ceased it was kept for six months and bottled for use.

Purl was a winter early morning drink, made from ale, a little rum or other spirits, with a little spice added. The whole was placed in a warmer over a fire and continuously stirred with a bunch of dried wormwood until sufficiently warm and bitter.

A visitor to Norfolk in the 19th century describes his first and only drink of purl: 'The natives are very fond of this tonic. On one occasion, two of my friends expressed their wish to try some. We accordingly adjourned to a tavern near Norwich, and ordered a glass each. It was made and brought in. "Good health!" was nodded by each to other, and a sip taken. No more! Each looked at the other with a look, as much as to say, "I'm poisoned", on his face.' One of his friends, a medical student, pronounced it 'the finest and most irresistible emetic he had ever tasted'. The other reckoned it was the 'devil's tipple'.

The brew was supposed to give you a wonderful appetite hence the Norfolk saying, 'A glass of purl before breakfast will make a man eat bricks'.

It was once customary on wealthy Norfolk farms to make a large quantity of cider of two qualities. At Christmas the best cider, which was often made one year in advance, was tapped for the family and so long as the Yule log was burning, which was usually for ten or twelve days, the servants had the 'common' cider. It was traditional to well dampen the huge log to make it burn more slowly and a small piece was always retained to light the next Yule log, this portion being known as the 'back log'. It was customary for the farmer and his family to take their meals with their servants during Christmastide.

On the morning of Christmas Day many farmers' wives cooked frumenty, which was given to the farm labourers and their families who were invited to the farmhouse for breakfast.

Frumenty looks unappetising but tastes delicious. It is made from wheat, raisins, currants, sugar, eggs and nutmeg, the whole lot simmered in milk and water. The wheat has first to be 'creed' or softened by placing it in a large dish filled with water and left in a low oven overnight.

Sadly nowadays if you feed your man too many apple dumplings he will think you are trying to kill rather than love him, for they are not cholesterol friendly. Children are no longer content to chomp on a Christmas pudding wrapper, which is probably all for the best. Good housewives are urged to feed their families rabbit, which is now very sound. There is no hint of 'bunny' to offend the sensitive, for it comes in perfect frozen dice, labelled 'high protein, low fat, guaranteed 95% pure lean meat'. The only hollow part is the ring of laughter coming from long departed farm servants.

Coke of Norfolk

IT was Thomas Coke's innovatory methods of farming from the late 18th century which helped turn the barren acres of North Norfolk into fertile land.

Popularly known throughout his life as Coke (pronounced 'Cook') of Norfolk, Thomas Coke, later the Earl of Leicester, inherited the 300,000 acre Holkham estate in 1776 when he was 22 years old. He was to become a long standing Whig MP, ending up as the Father of the House of Commons.

When he received his inheritance the estate was mainly rabbit infested land. People joked that these pests were the main 'cattle' to be found in this part of the county. The fields looked as if they had been ploughed by rabbits dragging knives behind them. If you saw one blade of grass you were more than likely to see two rabbits fighting over it!

The young man's policy was to give his tenants every possible encouragement to improve their farms, which he let to them on long leases with liberal covenants at an initial low rental. With such security they were likely to stay on his estates and become good tenants.

This part of Norfolk was one of the poorest agricultural parts of England. A little rye was grown and some 800 sheep with 'backs like rabbits' grazed with difficulty on 3,000 of his acres. It was almost impossible to keep cattle. The worthless soil took all the blame, but Coke replied that, 'Muck is the mother of money', and that with good nourishment the soil would become fruitful.

He picked the brains of neighbouring farmers and outside breeders to improve his lot and Robert Bakewell, a Leicestershire breeder, taught him how to judge an animal. Bakewell's cattle were reputed to be 'too dear for anyone to buy, and too fat for anyone to eat'. They were a prime example of good husbandry.

Coke's farming methods were based on the four-course system of husbandry devised at the end of the 17th century by the second Viscount 'Turnip' Townshend, whose estates were at Raynham, near Fakenham and fairly close to Holkham. This system using wheat, turnips, barley and clover, improved the fertility of the soil. The turnips were fed to the sheep who compacted the soil with their tiny feet and fertilised it with their waste.

Coke increased the number of sheep on his farms and after trying various breeds settled for Merinos and Southdowns. With Bakewell's guidance he imported and cross-bred local cattle with Devons. Animal manure was insufficient to fertilise all of his land so he caused great pits to be dug and covered the weak soil with rich marl subsoil. This clay did wonders and was quickly adopted by other farmers. Soon huge acreages of wheat and barley were waving over the entire district from Holkham to King's Lynn.

When the grasses were in flower Thomas Coke would show the village children examples of what he wanted and they would scour the countryside for the necessary seed. By this method good grasses and clover were made to flourish.

He next experimented with the drill on 3,000 acres of corn lands, which proved to be labour saving, economical with seed and it cleaned the land. Other machinery was introduced and instead of throwing his labourers out of work, more men were required and they were better paid. Three times the number of people were maintained on the same space as before. After experiment he introduced the use of oil cake, the growing of swedes and potatoes.

This landowner certainly was not afraid of hard work and was out in the fields from dawn to dusk, dressed in his smock, labouring as hard as any peasant. He travelled all over England to gain fresh ideas for improving his estate. He would return pleased that Norfolk was now at least no worse than many other counties of England, but often depressed by the ignorance and conservatism of the countryside. In Yorkshire he saw huge fertile meadows, beyond his wildest dreams, which grazed just one donkey. In Shropshire he reported riding many miles and seeing only two sheep, one being driven down the road and the other chained up in a field.

It was estimated that during his life he spent over half a million pounds upon his farms, cottages and buildings. When he commenced his farming career the annual gross rental from his estates was in the region of £2,000. In 1816 it amounted to £20,000. His tenants prospered alongside him and it was said his farmers 'lived like gentlemen, driving curricles and drinking port wine'. At the time of his inheritance the population of Holkham was under 200, by the end of the 19th century it had swelled to 1,100.

Annual sheep shearings were introduced at Holkham in 1778 and held for 45 years. They started off as a gathering for local farmers, to inspect the sheep and visit the home farm. However they evolved into huge three-day events and were the forerunner of today's agricultural shows. Visitors came from all over the country and from abroad to see how Coke's improved methods of farming worked, both on his farm and those of his tenants. It was claimed that the Holkham sheep shearings 'had indeed changed the habits and conditions of agricultural society'. Even William Cobbett, who disliked landlords, admitted that Coke was an exception. 'Everyone', he declared, after a visit to Holkham, 'made use of the expressions towards him which affectionate children use towards their parents.'

Thomas Coke died on 30th June, 1842, and was buried in the family vault at Tittleshall. There was an immense funeral procession, including most of the landowners and farmers of West Norfolk. A public subscription was raised for a monument to his memory and an obelisk was erected at Holkham Park. Reliefs represent the sheep shearings, the creation of an irrigation system, and the granting of a lease. A Southdown sheep, a Devon bull, a seed drill and a plough are shown on the four corners of the base. Some of Coke's friends and tenants who helped to make Holkham famous are also depicted on this monument to the Father of Norfolk farming, who converted a barren district into a granary.

Poppyland

O N 1st August 1883 Clement Scott, art critic, journalist and travel writer, then working with the *Daily Telegraph*, stepped off the London train at Cromer station and set about finding suitable accommodation whilst on a assignment to write about this new holiday town.

He was not pleased with the rooms on offer in Cromer, so leaving his luggage at the station he set off over the cliffs for a breath of fresh air, with nowhere in particular in mind. Little did he realise the importance of his invigorating stroll.

He eventually arrived at Overstrand, where he espied a red brick cottage with a beautiful garden opposite a windmill which stood on a small hill. He knocked on the door and enquired if by chance there were lodgings available. A girl of 19 replied that she had vacancies as her summer guests had just gone. The seeds of Poppyland were sown.

Louie Jermy, the miller's daughter who met him at the door, assured the middle aged journalist 'that her father would not quarrel about terms; that the fare at the farm was simple enough but that everyone would do their best for me'. Young Louie alone looked after her father and paying guests. She was a kindly shy girl, of meagre education but great intelligence, a good cook and housekeeper. As from that August day her life changed forever.

Scott returned to Cromer, collected his luggage, settled in comfortably at Mill House and set to work. On the 30th August 1883 his first 'pen picture' of the area was printed in the *Daily Telegraph* and proved so popular they became a regular feature. In 1886 by popular demand Jarrold & Sons of Norwich published them in book form entitled *Poppyland. Papers of Descriptive Scenery on the East Coast.*

In his first article he described his initial walk along the cliffs, 'It was on one of the most beautiful days in the lovely month of August, a summer morning with cloudless blue sky overhead and a sea without a ripple washing on the yellow sands. . . .' The mill house was 'a farmhouse within two fields of the sea, a garden full of flowers and fruit, a bedroom spotlessly clean with a full view of the windmill and the cornfields. . . .' Until his death the sentimental journalist was a frequent guest and always visited at harvest time when the coastal path and fields were ablaze with poppies.

At the bottom of Tower Lane near to his lodgings was an old church tower with the remains of a graveyard, all waiting to tumble over the rapidly eroding cliffs. The remainder of the 14th century church of St Michael, Sidestrand had been rebuilt further inland in 1880 to be safe from the inevitable drop. Scott was inexplicably drawn to this quiet spot with its magnificent views out to the North Sea, which he visited frequently. He never failed to return to the tower each New Year's Eve, to stand alone under the shadow of the tower to reflect upon the last dying moments of the old year.

In his spare time Scott wrote romantic and melodramatic poetry, which matched his style of journalism. His best poem was *The Garden of Sleep* which described the old tower and churchyard. He chose this name for reason of the eternal rest within the graveyard and the soporific poppies which flared over the dead at harvest time. The poem became an immediate success, was then put to music and sung in most music halls throughout the land. It was moreover a further inducement for people to come to 'Poppyland' whose poem they knew by heart:

The Garden of Sleep
(Subtitled '*A Summer Song*')

'On the grass of the cliff, at the edge of the steep,
God planted a garden — a garden of sleep!
'Neath the blue of the sky, in the green of the corn,
It is there that the regal red poppies are born!
Brief days of desire, and long dream of delight,
They are mine when my Poppy-Land cometh in sight.

In music of distance, with eyes that are wet,
It is there I remember, and there I forget!
O! heart of my heart! where the poppies are born,
I am waiting for thee, in the hush of the corn.
Sleep! Sleep!
From the Cliff to the Deep!
Sleep, my Poppy-Land,
Sleep!

In my garden of sleep, where red poppies are spread,
I wait for the living, alone with the dead!
For a tower in ruins stand guard o'er the deep,
At whose feet are green waves of dear women asleep!
Did they love as I love, when they lived by the sea?
Did they wait as I wait, for the days that may be?
Was it hope or fulfilling that entered each breast,
Ere death gave release, and the poppies gave rest?
O! life of my life! on the cliffs by the sea,
By the graves in the grass, I am waiting for thee!
Sleep! Sleep!
In the Dews by the Deep!
Sleep, my Poppy-Land,
Sleep!'

Its sentiment quickly set tongues wagging that he and Louie were putative lovers, especially as he kept his life in London with wife and children quite separate to that in Norfolk, his second home, even though Louie at a later date went into service with the Scotts for a brief period. The idea of the older man of 42 and a girl of 19 made good gossip but they persistently denied the rumours, Louie always referring to her paying guest as 'Mr Scott'.

Soon the journalist was bringing his friends to stay at the mill, Ellen Terry, Henry Irving, Algernon Swinburne and his boon companion Theodore Watts-Dunton, to name a few. Louie was attracted to the actors, poets and artists and enjoyed their regular company. In turn they were well content to be looked after by the willing Norfolk girl whose charming house and good simple cooking was the perfect antedote to their bohemian lives. Her speciality was blackberry pudding and her new friends dubbed her 'Louie of the Blackberry Puddings!'

The comings and goings and often outrageous behaviour of the Mill House guests caused quite a stir amongst the locals but Louie delighted in her circumstances having once had secret aspirations towards the stage herself. For a brief time one of her guests found her work in London as a dresser to an actress. She also received elocution lessons at the Royal School of Music, but Louie was a country girl and the pull of Overstrand brought her back to Poppyland. So Louie lived vicariously through the lives of her adored guests and gradually entered into her own dream world.

She followed their progress with care and faithfully read newspapers for any snippets of information. Hundreds of press cuttings were carefully put away along with other memorabilia. Sometimes for a special treat she went to London for a matinée.

Aided by the Great Eastern Railway and Scott's regular newspaper features, Poppyland became a popular resort. The train route became known as the 'Poppy Line' and in season disgorged bands of eager holidaymakers onto Cromer station. Happily lots were disinclined to move away from the town and its beach. The Mill House was known as 'Poppyland Cottage' and Louie 'The Maid of the Mill'. Overstrand became the 'Village of Millionaires' at the end of the 19th century when the rich and famous built their homes there. The population of the village soared from 253 to over 400 between the 1860s and 1890s.

Businessmen were not slow in exploiting Poppyland, which originally centred around Overstrand and Sidestrand and eventually extended to Great Yarmouth and Lowestoft, all resorts cashing in on the tourist boom and requiring new resources to service the visitors. Poppyland became a thriving industry. Hotels and boarding houses were quickly built and a large range of Poppyland china was brought out for souvenirs, all easily purchased from holiday budgets. There was a good selection of postcards printed by Jarrolds of Norwich and illustrated books and booklets commissioned on the famous scenery.

Various writers came to North Norfolk, many staying with Louie, all to write popular stories about the area, such as *Vera In Poppyland* by Mrs A. Berlyn who dedicated her work 'To my friend Clement Scott, the discoverer of Poppyland whose charming papers first led my steps to that peaceful haven, this little book is gratefully inscribed'. The Mill House intelligentsia often drew upon the area in their writing and dedications.

Poppyland mania began to fade with the death of Clement Scott in 1904 and some say that by 1912 it was almost finished. His friends erected a memorial fountain some five years after his death, which stands on the main Cromer to Overstrand road.

One morning in 1916 the tower and 'Garden of Sleep' toppled over the cliff without notice or witness, taking the bones of the 'sleepers' with them. Passersby had seen the tower as usual in the early morning and by lunchtime it had gone.

Despite her good looks and pleasing ways Louie never married. During the war her cottage became an officers' mess and canteen, which she took in her stride. After the war her guests were of a different ilk whom she found hard to keep in order.

In 1919 she was evicted from Mill House and moved to a cottage close by, which greatly saddened her. She lived alone and her last few years were spent as a sad old recluse selling blackberries from door to door and collecting junk in an old pram. Her new home was nicknamed 'The Old Curiosity Shop' for it was crammed full with memorabilia of her happy days and the hoardings of an old woman. Louie Jermy died in 1934, which signified the end of a link between the past and present.

At the time of writing the Mill House is still as Clement Scott described in his first article — apart from the addition of a front porch and being larger than imagined. It was 'A little red-brick house with three white windows on the first floor, a little white door in the middle, a window at each side, and a stack of chimneys at each end of the cottage.' The windmill has long gone and 'Four Winds' stands within the memory of its sails.

One of the saddest sights is a derelict bench seat inscribed, 'In Memory of Louie Jermy Poppyland 1934' which is teetering, frail and forgotten amongst some bramble bushes against the road a few yards opposite Mill House. It is an insult to her memory and the original spirit of Poppyland.

Louie's final cottage lies some 30 ft or so from the present cliff edge at the bottom of Tower Lane. Off to the right stood the old tower and 'The Garden of Sleep'. Even without Scott's arcadia it remains a beautiful almost spiritual place, with stunning views of the eroding cliffs and sandy beach with its sea groins stretching out like a giant steeplechase track. Even the most prosaic should be able to understand Clement Scott's love of the area.

The blackberry bushes so beloved of Louie Jermy and her pudding-eating friends continue to dangle their late summer fruit all along the roadside and down the lane to the cliffs. The stalwart harvest poppies flower with brilliance each year along the cliff tops and wherever man permits them room, unconscious of their ancestors' importance. The 'Maid of the Mill' and her guests have turned into legendary people and we are left with some words written by an unknown person concerning the lost tower and the 'Garden of Sleep':

'It has passed to the deep with its poppies of red,
Away on the cliffs desolation is spread,
For the Tower in ruins that guarded their sleep
Has passed with the poppies away to the deep.
I sigh as I look far away o'er the sea,
And think of the day that alas! ne'er can be.'

The Prostitutes' Padre

For over 30 years Harold Francis Davidson was the rector of Stiffkey cum Morston and lived at the Stiffkey rectory. His tremendous personality and bizarre lifestyle turned the little coastal village, at that time only famous for its Stewkey Blue cockles, into a newspaper reporter's dream. Rev Davidson supplied them with the main ingredients for selling tabloid newspapers: he was a bankrupt vicar connected with fallen women, show girls and a business venture which left many people out of pocket. After leaving Stiffkey his peculiar lifestyle continued to feed the presses of Fleet Street. Even his horrendous death made good copy.

This strange diminutive man, for he was only five feet three inches and nicknamed 'Little Jimmy' by his parishioners, is rapidly becoming absorbed into the folklore of Norfolk. He was born in a tough suburb of Southampton and his father, the vicar of Sholing assumed that his son would follow in the family footsteps and become the 28th Davidson to enter the Church.

Harold was none too sure for after leaving school he became a genteel stand-up comic, or to give him his rightful title, a 'drawing room entertainer', making his London debut in 1895.

During that time he rescued a young prostitute from committing suicide by drowning. She was only 16 years old, far from home and penniless and her plight was to become Davidson's lifelong mission — to save young girls aged between 14 and 20 years from a life of prostitution. It was later alleged that his relationship with some of the girls went far beyond the duties of a padre. Other ladies of the town testified that he was a kind man who never stepped out of line yet still gave them money out of his own pocket. Some regarded him as a saint and others a lecher who prayed on girls and yound women.

He commenced his ecclesiastic career at Oxford in 1898, combining show business with his studies. Two years before his graduation he became engaged to a hot tempered Irish actress called Molly Saurin, whom he married in 1906 when he took up his living at Stiffkey cum Morston.

They soon filled their 20-roomed rectory with paying and non-paying guests and in time there were four children to swell the numbers. It is said that Davidson took to going up to London six days a week to escape from Molly's fiery tongue. He was granted a special licence from his Bishop to undertake pastoral work outside his parish and was usually seen by his parishioners racing off the last train from London on a Saturday night.

It was a common sight on Sundays to see Harold Davidson bicycling furiously from one parish to the other, his cassock billowing out behind him. Often communion was taken without wine and baptisms conducted without water yet most of his flock tolerated his eccentricities and omissions with good grace. They used to joke that it was best not to die on a Monday for the corpse could get really 'high' waiting for the rector to return from London.

Rev Harold Davidson alias the Prostitutes' Padre's downfall had begun. He brought many of his 'filles de joie' back to the Stiffkey rectory for a Norfolk holiday much to the amazement and horror of some of the villagers. None of the rectory windows had curtains, which added to local speculation. Molly was furious to be landed with all these fallen women whom she called his 'lame cats'. In time their marriage was in name only and both led separate lives.

The London theatres drew Davidson like a magnet and in no time he became a chaplain working for the Actors' Church Union. Many said this Union was only an excuse for young vicars to rub shoulders with show girls but Little Jimmy took his role very seriously. Night after night he was to be found in their dressing rooms watching the costume changes, which got him banned from several theatres.

Still his parishioners waited patiently for their weddings, baptisms and burials. The villagers went about their daily tasks and in the main tolerated the strange crew living at the rectory. Davidson received a lot of local support in his time of trouble.

He is said to have started up an au pair agency for his London Ladies and took them to France to live with local families. This was open to interpretation, as was his partnership with Arthur John Gordon and their investment company which left many people severely out of pocket. The rector was declared bankrupt in 1925 when his living was halved to pay back his creditors.

He was hauled before the Lord Bishop of Norwich on several occasions, usually faring the better of the two. However, eventually charges were brought against him under the Clergy Discipline Act of 1892. After a long, salacious and well reported trial with many ladies of pleasure bearing witness for and against him, Davidson was defrocked. He lodged an appeal as was his right, but lost his case.

Stiffkey was over-run with the journalists who monitored poor Little Jimmy's every move. Three months lapsed between the court's decision and his final service. During this time he made heated sermons from his pulpit declaring his innocence and the treachery of the Church elders and gave long interviews to the press.

The 18th July 1932 edition of the *Daily Herald* reported the rector of Stiffkey making his debut at the Prince's Cinema in Wimbledon as a variety act between screenings of Lupe Velez in *The Storm*. On 9th August 1932 it was reported that Davidson had been thrown out of the Harrogate Sun-Bathing Society's premises when he tried to join in a game of nude medicine ball. He confided with the press that he was considering providing a similar sort of society amongst his parishioners at Stiffkey. The news hounds lapped it up!

His farewell service was held at Stiffkey on 21st August 1932 to a crowded congregation but Little Jimmy, still protesting his innocence, had more tricks to entertain them and keep Stiffkey firmly on the map.

He went off to Blackpool and became a carnival performer, earning very little money by undertaking strange and obnoxious acts to delight the holidaymakers. His new life started in a small barrel fitted out with an electric light, a seat and a tiny chimney through which he blew his cigar smoke. He lived and slept in it for a long time. He shouted to the holidaymakers through a little window that he was a wronged man. A sign was hung on the front of his dwelling which read, 'The former rector of Stiffkey has been placed in his present position by the authorities of the Church of England who failed in their Christian duty towards him. . . .'

Then he had a stint at being half frozen in a refrigerated chest and subsequently moved on to being half roasted in an oven with a mechanical devil prodding him in the backside with a fork to see if he were done. For a time he almost starved himself to death as a carnival act and a moral protest.

In between his shows he was put into prison for failing to pay his rent and other bad debts. He was further charged with pestering young girls, yet still he maintained that he was blameless and that the Church had wronged him.

His untimely death which followed a ghastly accident in a lions' cage surely befitted this strange attention-seeking little man, for it was such an uncommon ending. The main characters involved were a 'convent-educated' short-sighted 16 year old lion tamer named Irene Violet Somner and two lions, Freddie and his mate Toto. The date was 28th July 1937, and it happened in front of a large audience at Captain Rye's Pavilion at the Skegness Amusement Park.

Harold Davidson had delivered his customary ten minute speech to his audience whilst standing outside the lions' cage. It was the usual protest of personal innocence and the wretchedness of the Church authorities. He ended his discourse by saying that the day before the lions had been troublesome and he hoped that they would behave themselves that night. This was his nightly routine.

Although Freddie and Toto were docile creatures, Davidson was either doubly brave or foolish to do this act because he was basically terrified of all animals and went out of his way to avoid them.

That night Captain Rye, the owner of the show and most of this strong men were off duty. Irene, wearing her thick horn-rimmed glasses, stood by the closed door of the cage to watch his two to three minute performance. Her official role was to guard him with a starting pistol.

Davidson decided to give the lions a bit of a tickle with his whip, which annoyed Freddie but Toto did not stir. The lion became bored and seeking to put a stop to Harold's proddings he let out a great roar, reared upon his hind legs and knocked his tormentor to the floor. Then as an encore Freddie grabbed Harold by the scruff of his neck and stalked about the tiny cage shaking him like a cat with a mouse. For a brief second the audience howled with laughter thinking it was part of the act, then they screamed with horror and rushed from the pavilion.

Violet stormed into the cage, lost her spectacles and dropped the starting pistol in the sawdust. Being almost as blind as a bat without her glasses she fumbled around, picked up a tree branch lying on the floor and proceeded to hit the lion. This stirred Toto into life and she too had her sport. Eventually the brave girl dragged Harold out of the cage and he died a few days later.

There was still mileage to be had from Little Jimmy. Various limericks, jokes and songs had already been written about the vicar of Stiffkey, the latter word usually having a double meaning. Davidson had successfully sued one gramophone company and received £350 compensation for a wicked song which had been sold in Woolworths. More of the same flooded the market after his death.

He became the hero of two musicals, which were both flops. The first entitled *The Vicar of Soho* was performed at the Stables Theatre, Manchester, in 1969 and later *The Stiffkey Scandals of 1932* folded after nine days at the Queen's Theatre, London.

Harold Francis Davidson is buried in the churchyard at Stiffkey. His headstone is facing the wrong way and is inscribed with a quotation from Robert Louis Stevenson: 'For on faith in man and genuine love of man all searching after truth must be founded.' Time has obliterated Davidson's name from the stone, but it remains in the hearts of many of his old parishioners who agree that 'Little Jimmy were a rum ol' boy!'

Kett's Rebellion

FOR some time before the Norfolk uprising in 1549, labourers had been whispering to one another that better times were coming and that:

> 'The country gnoffes, Hob, Dick and Hick,
> With clubbs and clouted shoon,
> Shall fill the vale of Dussin's Dale
> With slaughtered bodies soon.'

Little did they realise that this was a two edged prophecy and it would be their bodies filling the vale.

John Flowerdew, Sergeant at Law, was commissioned to supervise the pulling down of the monastic buildings at Wymondham. He was loathed for his actions and overpowering manner. The local people had organised a public subscription to purchase parts of the abbey church used by the monks, and Robert Kett, a master tanner, was one of the biggest subscribers. The money was handed over to the authorities and their consent to the scheme was obtained. Flowerdew ignored the agreement and proceeded to strip the church. He further added to the tension when he enclosed some common land at Hethersett.

On 25th June 1549 there was a riot at Attelborough when the new enclosures and fences which had been illegally erected on common land by Squire Green were pulled down.

The next landmark was the annual Feast of Wymondham, Sunday 7th July, when the old guild play to commemorate St Thomas à Becket was performed. A large crowd gathered, speeches were made and the next day all of Flowerdew's enclosures were razed to the ground. Robert Kett and his brother

William, described as either a butcher or tanner from Wymondham, were part of the mob.

Flowerdew went to Wymondham and offered the men 40 pence to knock down the fences which Kett, who was also a landowner, had installed around some common land at Fairstead. Kett was told about Flowerdew's proposition. There was great enmity between the two men and the former is said to have replied, 'Whatsoever lands I have enclosed shall again be made common unto ye and all men, and my own hands shall first perform it.' He then led them in the demolition of his own fences.

The peasants urged Robert Kett to become the leader of what was to become a movement to curb the tryannical power of the gentry and improve the lot of the labouring classes. He proved to be a born leader and it was his belief that he was fighting for the law and not against it, for most of the enclosures and depopulations were illegal.

By degrees the insurgents journeyed to Bowthorpe where they were ordered by the High Sheriff to disperse, but in fear of his own life, he decided to run away.

Eventually Robert Kett set up camp at Mousehold Heath, north-east of Norwich, where other rebels had gathered before. Soon some 20,000 men were ready for action. Lesser camps were formed at Rising Chase and at Downham there was until the last century a tree named 'Kett's Oak'. However these gatherings were of little effect.

A chaplain joined the men at Mousehold and conducted regular services. Rations were foraged from the city and cattle were moved into the encampment for food. Provisions were brought in from as far away as Yarmouth and Lynn.

Kett formed a committee of management which met under a large oak tree on Mousehold Heath, which was to become known as the 'Tree of Reformation'. Thomas Codd, beer brewer and mayor of Norwich, Thomas Aldridge, draper, and a past mayor of the city, were co-opted onto the committee.

A petition was then sent to the King's Council which set out their reasonable demands. Besides various clauses against enclosures it asked redress against lords of manors who tried to make their freehold tenants pay their own head-rent and castle-guard rent, which they considered should be the outgoings of the lords and not their tenants. It asked that all 'bondmen' should be made free, 'for God made all free with His precious blood shedding', that all rivers should be made free and common to all men for fishing and passage; that parsons should be resident and all having a benefice worth more than £10 a year, 'shall by himself or deputy, teach the poor parish children the catechism and the primer.' In the interest of their crops they sought that no one under a certain degree should keep rabbits unless he 'paled' them in and that no new dove-houses should be allowed. The document bore the signatures of Kett, Codd and Aldridge.

The sting of the whole thing was the demand for throwing open enclosures, made to lords of manors of waste land over which their tenants had commonable rights.

The petition received no positive consideration by the authorities, who had some half a dozen minor risings already on their hands. All that happened was that the King's herald went to the camp by Kett's permission and tried to put a stop to further action. Kett insisted from first to last that he was there to uphold the law and not to break it and replied that 'Kings were wont to pardon wicked persons, not innocent and just men.'

Thomas Codd, the mayor of Norwich and one of the signatories to Kett's petition, became angered by the former's rebuffal of the King's representative and barred him from the city. This forced Kett's army into action. Norwich was attacked and Codd taken prisoner. A grim joke was soon put about that anyone coming to Mousehold would soon get a cod's head for a penny, but in time he was set free.

The citizens bravely guarded the walls and fortifications of their city and showered Kett's men with arrows. 'Vagabond boys, naked and unmarked, came among the thickest of the arrows and gathered them up, and plucked out the very arrows that were sticking in their bodies, and gave them, all dripping with blood, to the rebels who were standing by, to fire against the city.' The rebels took Norwich. There was no looting and Kett had assumed that the Norwich people would be for their cause but in the main they were not.

At last the King's army, under the Marquess of Northampton, came to the aid of Norwich. He brought 2,500 men, many being

Italian mercenaries. One of the Italians was captured, stripped of his armour and hanged upon an oak, though £100 was offered for his ransom. Lord Sheffield was slain close to the cathedral and a plaque marks the spot.

The government sent more reinforcements and the Earl of Warwick came with some 12,000 trained men including 1,000 German mercenaries with fire-arms.

Terms were once more made to Kett and refused. There followed terrible fighting in the one acre city battle ground. The next day 320 of Kett's men were killed and many others 'found creeping in the churchyards and under the walls' were knocked on the head.

Parts of the city were on fire and the rebels removed to Mousehold Heath where they made their fatal mistake. They relied on the old prophecy that if they occupied Dussin's Vale all would be well. Kett burned down his strong encampment and took his men down to the lower ground near the Wensum where he took up a defensive position.

Their change of direction was notified to Warwick by his lookout on the cathedral spire and his massive number of troops headed for Dussin's Dale. The whole thing was soon over. Kett's untrained men, who had fought gallantly in the narrow streets and lanes, were overpowered when they found themselves butchered wholesale in the open. Some 3,500 men were simply murdered and the cruelty and carnage was so great they just stood together in confused groups determined to die fighting.

Revenge was great and the hangings went on for days. The gentry who had suffered from damage to their enclosures, but had themselves remained unharmed, screamed for blood. In the end Warwick was forced to declare, 'Is there no place for pardon? Shall we hold the plough ourselves, and harrow our own lands?'

Kett and his brother William were taken to London for trial, brought back to Norfolk and Robert was hanged from a gibbet erected on the tower of Norwich Castle. William was hanged from the church tower of Wymondham.

In 1949 a memorial plaque was placed on Norwich Castle '. . . in reparation and honour to a notable and courageous leader in the long struggle of the common people of England to escape from a servile life into the freedom of just conditions.'

Jack O'Lantern

J ACK o' Lantern or Will o' the Wisp were two of the names given to little flickers of marsh gas thought by many to be evil spirits waiting to lure lone night travellers to their death. In fact they were the spontaneous combustion of marsh gas which occurred on warm nights in rotten swamps and bogs. Better drainage has now turned these apparitions into memories. Some people called them Corpse Candles, other Hob o' Lanterns or Jenny Burnt Arses.

According to Mrs Lubbock, a 19th century wise woman from Irstead, near Neatishead, Jack o' Lantern was often to be seen walking around her village before the Irstead enclosure of 1810.

Irstead remains an isolated village standing close to the river Ant, but unlike Mrs Lubbock's time it is now a very desirable place in which to live with parts looking like an archetypal English village. It has held on to lots of its thatched cottages and its church with a similar roofing material is a delight. Until this century's gentrification and better methods of drainage it would have been a very damp and unhealthy place, miles removed from civilisation. No wonder such communities seethed with tales of the supernatural and paranormal.

Mrs Lubbock's account of Jack o' Lantern was of the spirit of a man named Heard, who turned into a Lantern Man and was frequently seen in the village on a 'roky' (misty) night and almost always at a place called Heard's Holde, in Alder Carr Fen Broad, on the Neatishead side. There a man of that name who was guilty of many horrendous crimes was drowned. She said, 'I have often seen it there, rising up and falling and twistering about, and then up again. It looked exactly like a candle in a lantern.' She obviously connected the 'ignus fatuus' in that spot with the unhappy man's spirit, as if it were still hovering about. 'If anyone were walking along the road with a lantern at the time when he appeared and did not put out the light immediately, Jack could come against it and dash it to pieces, and that a gentleman who made a mock of him, and called him, "Will o' the Wisp", was riding on horseback one evening in the adjoining parish of Horning, when he came at him and knocked him off his horse.'

She further remembered that as a child her father had said that once when he was returning from a largesse money-spending at the end of harvest, in company with an old man who whistled and jeered at Jack, the spirit followed them home and when they entered the house he 'torched up' at the windows.

The local people were keen to lay Heard's spirit, which came to them at certain times and to places which he had frequented when alive. Three men tried to exorcise the ghost by reading verses of the Scripture, but he always kept a verse ahead of them, and they could do nothing until a boy brought a couple of pigeons and laid them down before the apparition. He looked down at the birds and lost his verse, and then they 'bound his spirit'.

The danger of Lantern Men is further illustrated in this tale from Cromer as told by an old fisherman which appeared in Volume 1 of the *Eastern Counties Magazine* in 1900:

'There's no saying what that will du to you, if that light on you! There was a young fellow coming home one evening and he see the Lantern Man coming for him and he run; and that run and he run again; and that run again! Now there was a silly old man lived down there who didn't believe in none o' them things and this young fellow he run to his house and say, "O Giles, for Heaven's sake, let me in — the Lantern Man's coming!" And old Giles he say, "You silly fool, there ain't no such thing as a Lantern Man." But when he see the Lantern Man coming for him, Giles let the young fellow in, and that come for them two, till that was the beginner of a pint pot!

'And old Giles, he thought he would play a trick on the Lantern Man so he got a candle and held that out right high; and the Lantern Man, he come right low and the Lantern Man he come up above it. And then he held out right steady, and the Lantern Man he come for that and he burst it all to pieces.

'But they du say, if the Lantern Man light upon you, the best thing is to throw yourself flat on your face and hold your breath.'

Norfolk Lavender

L AVENDER bags, water, soap, oil, furniture polish, air freshener, pot-pourri, nursery rhymes and cottage gardens. There can be few people who do not love this fragrant plant. Perhaps its scent brings back memories of their mother's energetic polishing, or granny's perfume when she planted a kiss on a young face? Or perhaps her chest of drawers where she kept her best linen comes to mind, or her dark and mysterious wardrobe, for many grandmothers knew the wisdom of the rhyme:

'Velvet gown and dainty fur
Should be laid in lavender,
For its sweetness drives away
Fretting moths of silver grey.'

It is thought that the Romans, who put a lot of faith in lavender's healing and insect repellant properties, brought it with them when they conquered Britain. Its name is derived from the Latin word *lavendum*, which translates as 'fit for washing'. Roman public baths were perfumed with lavender and their gods honoured with the perfume of the burnt flower. The Romans used the oil for massage and it continues to play a major part in aromatherapy world wide.

In the 14th century Charles VI of France relaxed on white satin lavender cushions and the Tudors discovered that when mixed with beeswax it made an ideal polish to prevent wood infestation. Their newly introduced tobacco was enhanced with lavender mixture, both for smoking and snuff, and similar recipes are still available. During this period lavender and charcoal was used as a tooth cleanser and Queen Elizabeth I was fond of lavender conserve, made by steeping the flowers in sugar.

John Gerard, the famous herbalist of that time, advised in his *Historie of Plants* that, 'The floures of Lavender picked from the knaps, I meane the blew part and not the husk, mixed with Cinnamon, Nutmegs, & Cloves, made into pouder, and given to drinke in the distilled water thereof, doth help the panting and passion of the heart, prevaileth against giddinesse, turning, or swimming of the braine, and members subject to the palsie.' Many doctors and herbalists continue to enthuse over the plant's healing properties which have many applications.

It was in the 17th century that lavender oil was mixed with soap to overcome the awful rancid smell of fat. Bundles of flowers were burnt in halls and public places to cleanse the air during the Great Plague of 1665 and as a consequence the price of lavender soared. For many centuries the call of 'Sweet blooming lavender' mingled with the myriad cries to be heard in towns and cities throughout the land.

If you are lucky enough to be near Heacham and its surrounding area in early July and August, you will be dazzled by the wonderful scent and colour of acres of lavender fields, lying under a sea-bright sky.

Norfolk Lavender Ltd, based at Caley Mill, Heacham, is the sole remaining large-scale lavender farm in England and has scented the countryside for nearly 60 years.

The Norfolk story began in 1874 when Linn Chilvers started a florist's business and nursery gardens at Heacham. He was the son of a successful botanist who supplied plants to Queen Alexandra for her Sandringham gardens and both father and son were interested in lavender and grew several varieties. Local farmers believed that the plant depleted the soil of nourishment, but the Chilvers proved them wrong. Norfolk offered the right conditions and in 1932 Linn Chilvers went into partnership with Ginger Dusgate of Fring Hall.

Dusgate provided the six acres of land at Fring and Chilvers the 13,000 plants. The planting, which cost a total of £15, took three men and a boy 18 days to complete. The first crop was harvested the following year.

Not long after the partnership was formed Mr Avery, a

Leicester chemist with a special interest in perfumery, called on the nursery. He had a recipe for a lavender perfume made for King George IV in the early 19th century.

For many years the chemist visited Norfolk to mix his secret essences and the formula was eventually purchased by the partnership. The perfume was bottled and labelled by Linn's two sisters, Violet and Ivy, in an old wooden bungalow at the nursery, and sold from the kiosk in the nursery gardens and local chemists.

After the Second World War a disease called Shab almost wiped out the old lavender fields in southern England and the farms around London sold off their land for urban development. With good husbandry the Norfolk fields have expanded to some 100 acres which are now directed by the Head family, Linn Chilvers having died in 1953.

Norfolk Lavender and Caley Mill with its little kiosk painted out in lavender colour cannot be separated.

Part of the mill garden is given over to the National Collection of Lavender, established under the auspices of the National Council for the Conservation of Plants and Gardens, a registered charity based at Wisley Gardens. The purpose of the collection is for the classification of lavender and is seasonally open to the public.

Norfolk lavender plays an important role within the county. As no harmful pesticides are said to be used, the fields abound with wildlife. Partridges nest amongst the bushes and in summertime the acreage is alive with butterflies and honey bees. Visitors come to experience first hand the pleasures offered at Caley Mill, an archetypal part of 'Olde England'. All this stems from the original venture made by two Norfolkmen who were determined to succeed. Linn Chilvers, the founder of the company has not been forgotten, for his signature is to be found on every Norfolk Lavender product.

'Here Lies Will Salter, Honest Man'

Tombstones and church memorials can be an interesting source of local history. At St Mary's church, Heacham, tribute is paid to Pocahontas, a Red Indian princess and daughter of Chief Powhatan, who married John Rolfe from Heacham Hall in 1614. It was she who intervened to save the lives of some Norfolk settlers in Virginia during the early days of the American colonies. The couple returned to England and Pocahontas became a sought after part of London society. Sadly just before they were due to sail back to America in 1617 she died. The princess was only 22 years old and our climate did not agree with her.

Hidden by the organ at St Mary's, Martham, in the Norfolk Broads is a memorial to Christopher and Alice Burraway which has all the ingredients of a modern soap opera. It states that Alice, 'by hir life was my sister, my mistress, my mother and my wife.' Alice died at the age of 76 in 1729. Christopher followed her the next year aged 59 years.

The traditional explanation for this enigmatic statement is that Alice bore a child (she was a mother) by an incestuous relationship with her father (so a sister). The child was passed off as an orphan to avoid scandal but returned as a man to become the steward of his sister/mother's farm (so Alice was his mistress). Later they were wed (so a wife). Another less scandalous view is that Christopher Burraway married his step-father's widow, who filled for him all the roles described on the memorial.

The tomb of Robert Hales, the 'Norfolk Giant' can still be seen in the ancient chuchyard at West Somerton, near Great Yarmouth. Robert was born in that parish in 1820, the son of a local farmer. Both his parents were uncommonly tall, and he grew to a height of seven ft eight inches and weighed over 32 stone. Accompanied by his sister Mary who was also over seven ft tall, he appeared at fairs and shows throughout the country and in 1848 visited the United States of America. On returning to England he became licensee of the Craven Head tavern in London where his great height attracted a lot of customers. He was presented to Queen Victoria and was well known for his gentle manner and kindness. Robert Hales died at Great Yarmouth in 1863.

The churchyard of the priory and parish church of St Nicholas at Great Yarmouth has two especially interesting grave stones. To the west is recorded at length the death of a young seaman and his mate by a notorious pirate.

'To The Memory of David Bartleman
Mafter of the Brig Alexander and Margaret North Shields
who on the 31st Jan 1781 on the Norfolk Coast
with only three 3 pounders and ten
Men and Boys
Nobly defended himself Againft a Cutter carrying eighteen 4
pounders
an upwards of a Hundred Men
Commanded by the notorious English Pirate
Fall
and fairly beat him off
2 hours after the Enemy came down upon him again
when totally disabled his Mate
Daniel MacAuley
expiring with the loss of blood
and himfelf dangerously wounded
he was obliged to strike and ransome
He brought his shattered Vefsel into Yarmouth
With more
than the Honours of a Conqueror
and died here in consequence of his wounds
on the 14th February following

in the 25th year of his Age.
To Commemorate the Gallantry of his Son
the Bravery of his faithful mate
and at the same time mark the Infamy of
a
Savage Pirate
his afflicted Father Alexander Bartleman
has ordered this Stone to be erected
over his
Honourable Grave
T'was Great his Foe tho strong was infamous
(the foe of human kind)
A many indignation fired his Breaft
That God my son has done his Duty.'

Opposite the south porch is the gravestone of a young boy who was drowned when the Haven Suspension Bridge collapsed killing many people. It was on a fine afternoon in May 1845 that a crowd of people swarmed onto the suspension bridge which straddled the river Bure. They were gathered to watch a clown called Nelson sailing down the river in a tub drawn by four geese. The weight of all the people being on one side of the bridge broke the chains and everything crashed into the water. At the top of the child's memorial is a carving of the collapsed bridge with the eye of God above, looking down on the drowning people:

'To the Memory of
George H. J. Belloe
The Beloved Son of
Louisa Belloe
Who was unfortunately drowned
by the fall
of the Suspension Bridge
The 2nd of May 1845
Aged 9 Years.
Farewell dear Boy no more I press
Thy form of light and loveliness
And those who gazed on thy sweet face
Knew it to be an angels dwelling place

'HERE LIES WILL SALTER, HONEST MAN'

And of that realm where thou art now
Be filled with beings such as thou
From sin set free and sorrow freed
then Heaven must be a Heaven indeed.'

There are lots of interesting and amusing epitaphs scattered around the county. Take for instance that of Will Salter, an 18th century coachman who regularly drove from Yarmouth to Cambridge. He was killed when his coach turned over on the steep hill against Haddiscoe church, where he is buried in the churchyard. His memorial is set in the church wall:

'Here lies Will Salter, honest man,
Deny it, Envy, if you can;
True to his business and his trust,
Always punctual, always just.
His horses could they speak would tell
they lov'd their good old master well.
His up-hill work is chiefly done;
His stage is ended. Race is run,
One journey is remaining still,
To climb up Zion's holy hill.
And now his faults are all forgiv'n,
Elijah-like drives up to heav'n;
Takes the reward for all his pains,
And leaves to other hands the reins.'

Robert Gilbert of the parish of Cantley, a country gentleman and huntsman, died on 5th November 1714. His inscription is to be found set in the floor of the chancel of St Margaret's church.

'In wise frugality luxuriant
In justice and good acts extravagant,
To all the world an universal friend,
No foe to any but the savage kind.
How many fair estates have been eras'd
By the same gen'rous means that his increas'd.
His duty thus perform'd to heaven and earth,
Each leisure hour fresh toilsom sports gave birth;

Had Nimrod seen he would the game decline,
To Gilbert's might hunter's name resign.
Tho' hundreds to the ground he oft has chas'd,
That subtle fox Death earth'd him here at last,
And left a fragrant scent so sweet behind
that ought to be pursu'd by all mankind.'

Sadly weather and lichen are making some of these old stones for the most part illegible. Their loss will be considerable.

Mary Smith's
Flying Heart

A BOVE a first floor window of No 15 Tuesday Market Place at
King's Lynn, there is a small diamond shape cut into the
brickwork enclosing a heart shaped mark. From the gallows a
local witch, Mistress Mary Smith, predicted that her heart would
burst from her body and fly above the window of the magistrate
who had convicted her, and this is where it is supposed to have
landed.

The fact that the incident is supposed to have taken place in the
17th century, some 100 years before the present building was
erected, adds to the improbability that a heart could imbed itself
into a wall.

It was on 12th January 1616 that Mary was executed on the
charge of witchcraft, to the indignation of many people. James I
had not long repealed the Elizabethan statutes which had made it
an offence only to kill by witchcraft. The new enactment made it a
capital offence, 'If any person or persons shall use, practise or
exercise an Invocation or Conjuration of any evill and wicked
Spirit, or shall consult, covenant with, entertaine, employ, feede
or rewarde any evill and wicked Spirit to or for any purpose; or
take up any dead man, woman, or child out of his, her or their
grave, or any place where the dead body resteth, or the skin, bone
or any part of any dead person to be employed or used in any
manner of witchcraft, enchantment, charm or sorcerie, whereby
any person shall be killed, destroyed, wasted, consumed, pined,
or lamed in his or her body, or any part thereof, every such
offender is a felon without benefit of clergy.'

Rev Alexander Roberts, who took part in the trial, tried to justify the same by publishing a full account of the proceedings. Its title page reads as follows:—

'A Treatise of Witchcraft, Wherein Sundry propositions are laid downe, plainly discovering the Wickednesse of that damnable Art, with a True Narration of the Witchcrafts which Mary Smith, wife of Henry Smith, Glover, did practice: Of her contract vocally made between the Devill and her, in Solemne Termes, by whose means she hurt sundry persons whom she envied: which is confirmed by her owne confession, and also from the Publique Records of the Examination of diverse upon their oathes: And lastly of her death and execution, for the same; which was on the twelfth day of Jannarie last past, by ALEXANDER ROBERTS, B.D., and Preacher of God's Word at King's-Linne in Norffolke, Exod.22.18. Thou shalt not suffer a Witch to live. . . . London: Printed by N.O. for Samvel Man, and are to be sold at his shop in Paul's Churchyard at the signe of the Ball, 1616.'

It would appear that despite the efforts of the loathed Matthew Hopkins, the Witchfinder-General and his fellow 'Witch Prickers' who terrorised East Anglia from 1644 to 1647, no more men or women of King's Lynn were executed for witchcraft.

The devil in the form of a black man is alleged to have appeared before Mary and promised her wonderful things if she renounced God. This she did and became endowed with the power of witches to curse people.

Her first victim was John Orkton, a sailor, who had hit her son. She told him that his fingers would drop off as a punishment. He was ill for some nine months and his fingers and toes became gangrenous and had to be amputated.

Mary believed that widow Elizabeth Hancock had stolen one of her hens and cursed the woman. She became very ill and visitors saw her bed levitate. Elizabeth Hancock firmly believed that she had been bewitched by Mary Smith and her father, Edward Drake, could no longer bear the sight of his daughter in pain and torment. He consulted a 'cunning man' from Great Yarmouth who told Edward Drake as soon as he arrived that he knew that he was seeking help for his daughter and added that she was so worn down by her affliction that if she remained in that condition for just one more day she would die. He also showed Drake the face of his daughter in a looking glass and told him that the witch had accused Elizabeth Hancock of stealing her hen.

He then gave the father the following directions which, if strictly followed, would relieve the woman from her bewitchment.

'Make a cake with flour from the baker's, and mix with the same the patient's urine instead of other liquor, and bake it on the hearth. One half of this cake to be laid on the patient about the region of the heart, and the other half to be applied to the back directly opposite.'

He also gave a box of ointment, which looked like treacle, which had to be spread upon the cake, and a powder to be sprinkled over it and certain words written on a paper which had to be laid on top of the cake.

Edward Drake was told that if his daughter did not show signs of improvement within six hours of the adoption of this remedy then there was no further help for her. He also emphasised that silence should be kept, 'as the woman, it is said, was by this means freed from the languishing torments that she had endured for a week.'

Urine and silence were common ingredients for getting rid of a hex, the former often being put in a glass or clay 'witch's bottle' along with pins and red thread to resemble blood, well stoppered and put into the fire. The urine and 'blood' represented a personal link between the bewitched and the bewitcher, this being a vital part of witchcraft. As the liquid boiled and so long as silence was maintained until the end of the operation, the witch would soon get an excruciating pain in her stomach or another organ and beg for the bottle to be taken from the fire in return for the removal of the curse or bewitchment.

Two more people were cursed before Mary Smith was dragged off to prison and subsequently hanged in Tuesday Market Place and her heart flew into the wall.

It is quite probable that the reason for Mistress Smith's death was simple minded hysteria and coercion rather than the 'witchcraft' evinced by the 'Preacher of God's word at King's Linne.' Irrespective of the cause of the mark, it remains yet another symbol of the sinister side of mankind.

Looking at
the Broads

THE Norfolk Broads are shallow lakes or meres which lie alongside the rivers Waveney, Yare and Bure and their tributaries. It is believed that these lakes are the flooded remains of peat diggings which took place between the 12th and 15th centuries.

Peat was the main local source of fuel before it was supplanted by sea coal. For centuries Great Yarmouth supplied Europe with salted herring, the season lasting from September to Decenber. It is thought the salt was taken from the sea and peat used to heat the brine baths. The fish industry had a readily available source of energy with a good network of waterways for its transportation.

The shallow waters were ideal for barge traffic, the earliest known type being the Norfolk Keel, a double ended craft with a square keel. From the 18th century this was superseded by the Norfolk Wherry which carried a single gaff sail which allowed it to sail close to the wind.

In the hey-day of the wherry trade the men had a standard way of greeting each other when going up and down the river. One boat would call out, 'There you go!' and the other replied, 'There you blow!'

Like most people working in a close group, the wherrymen had their standard jokes about idiotic colleagues such as, 'Have you heard about the wherryman who dropped a kettle overboard while sailing? He ran to the side of the boat and cut a "snotch" with his knife to mark the spot so that he would be able to find it later on!'

From the middle of the 19th century it was becoming fashionable for people to hire pleasure-wherries instead of yachts. They were obviously far more suited to exploring the Norfolk Broads and offered more cabin space. They could be hired for about £7 10s a week. One writer thought the fashion might spread!

Those hiring the pleasure-craft were advised to take some vinegar in which their lamp wicks should be soaked and then thoroughly dried. This would prevent the usual unpleasant smoky oil lamps which could ruin a pleasant jaunt.

They were also given a recipe for waterproofing their boots before setting off. They should place half a pound of tallow to quarter pound of resin in a pot on the fire. When thoroughly melted it was applied to warm boots, laid on with a painter's brush until the sole and uppers were thoroughly saturated. Twenty four hours later the boots should be shined up with one ounce of wax mixed with a little lampblack.

In the late 19th century it was pointed out that although Wroxham might be the headquarters of Norfolk yachting, from the convenience of the railway station and being surrounded by some of the prettiest scenery, it had a very bad supply of shops and 'other victualling accommodation'. Would-be sailors were reminded to stock up on food and drink because, 'except by accident, when one may get fowls and eggs, there is no place between Wroxham and Yarmouth where eatable food or drinkable drink can certainly be obtained.'

Inexperienced sailors were told to beware of unseen danger which was peculiar to Norfolk. This was 'Roger', the name given to a whirlwind which occasionally struck yachts sailing on the Broads, before the crew was aware of its approach. By keeping a good look-out you could see the reeds and trees along the river-side become violently agitated. Quick steps to trim the sails prevented sailors from being harmed by 'Roger', who was responsible for the drowning of three experienced men at the Wroxham Regatta in 1881 whilst a tent on shore was taken up in the air and carried a distance of 80 yards.

Visitors gliding down the Broads in the early spring, even during the early part of this century, would see and hear small boys in charge of several fields, scaring birds who were bent on feeding off the barley and late wheat sowings. The boy would first make a loud noise with his wooden clapper, three pieces of wood joined with a piece of string so they banged together. He then started his 'war' song which always ended in true Red Indian fashion with a war cry. Here is the Norfolk bird-boys' song:

'Cadders and crows, take care of your toes,
For here come the clappers,
To knock you down backwards:
So, hallo! Carwho! wo! who!! whoop!!!'

During the 19th century the spring and summer wild flowers in the reaches of the Bure between Horning and Wroxham, and even as far as Aylsham, blazed with vibrant colour. A writer commented that a friend of his had taken some albums with her on her journey and had pressed some of the flowers. 'It was wonderful what pretty results were obtained by a little patience and skill in arranging these specimens. This is a hint for ladies who wish to know how to fill up their spare time.' Spare time should now be filled in other ways as picking wild flowers is a criminal activity.

Fishing reached its height in August and offered good sport for the chaps, who were reminded that the morning swim should never be omitted, and should be indulged in early before the ladies were about. They were to take the jolly-boat or dinghy, pull to a secluded spot and indulge in a delightful bathe to their heart's content and body's welfare. However it was important to wait for any early mist to clear for a bathe in such vapour was dangerous to health.

September was the time for visitors to do a spot of eel catching. Night lines were permitted, providing they were not armed with more than one hook, and some good hauls could be made by those who had the patience to bait and lay a couple of dozen lines. During the late 19th century most of the eels were bought up by one Yarmouth firm who sent boats to the various rivers and Broads and collected them from their eel 'sets' or netting stations.

This month was also the start of the shooting season, much to the delight of the retriever dogs employed to recover the birds which had fallen into the reed ronds.

Mushrooms grew aplenty in certain marshes, especially if the weather was fine with just a little rain. As one writer observed, 'What a place for an epicure: tender juicy steaks and mushrooms for a relish, growing on the same marsh!'

The Broadlands were a popular place in freezing weather, when skaters could zoom over hundreds of acres of frozen, flooded, shallow marshes, and those who wished could take part in skating matches.

Winter was also the time for the wildfowlers who put iron runners on their punts to get them over the ice. The boats were filled with animal fodder, or marsh hay for the men to lie upon and keep warm. In the forepart they built a screen of rushes, furze or twigs, with a peep hole and an arrangement of crossed sticks upon which to rest their punt guns. These were muzzle-loaders with enormously long barrels and looked as dangerous to the sportsmen as to the birds.

The Norfolk Broads continue to provide the right environment for growing the marvellous Norfolk Reed or *phragmites communis*, considered to be the best form of thatching material, both for a weather-tight covering and for durability. A Norfolk reed roof should last up to 70 years, except for the ridge which is usually made out of flexible wheat straw which needs renewing every twelve years. The beds are scattered all over the Broads, some are the property of commercial suppliers, others being owned by or rented out to thatchers.

There are still many houses with thatched roofs in Norfolk as well as a number of thatched churches. After a disastrous fire at Norwich in 1507 in which 718 houses were destroyed, future thatched buildings were prohibited. Happily the 'Barking Dicky' in the Giles Jolterhead ballad still retains its thatch, but is no longer a hostelry.

Little did the ancient peat cutters realise that their industry would pave the way for such an important and unique future legacy, not just for nature but also for man in his many moods.

Norwich Joes
and
Yarmouth Bloaters

NORFOLK is rich in place nicknames, rhymes and prophecies which are well worth recording as part of old county tales. These jingles would sometimes be used to taunt the folks from over the border!

King's Lynn was not known by its present name until it was surrendered by the Bishop of Norwich to Henry VIII, when it was renamed Lynn Regis or King's Lynn. Until that time it was Bishop's Lynn or Len Episcopi, 'Len' meaning a farm. The town is teased in the rhyme:

> 'That nasty, stinking, sink-hole of sin,
> Which the map of the county denominates Lynn.'

Visitors to Castle Rising, which is not far from King's Lynn, would never believe that it was once an important sea port as it now stands several miles inland. It was thriving when Lynn was nothing, as told in the verse:

> 'Rising was a seaport town,
> And Lynn it was a waste,
> But Lynn it is a seaport town,
> And Rising fares the worse.'

Local prophecies are contained in verse:

> 'Rising was, Lynn is, and Downham shall be,
> The greatest seaport of the three.'
> (The latter is well inland.)

> 'Gorleston, great one day will be;
> Yarmouth, buried in the sea.'

> 'He who would old England win,
> Must at Weybourne Hoop begin.'

> ''Twixt Lopham Ford and Shrimpling Thorn,
> England shall be won and born.'

Some rhymes run delightfully off the tongue such as the geographical:

> 'Gimingham, Trimingham,
> Knapton and Trunch,
> Northrepps and Southrepps,
> All in a bunch.'

The poet Swinburne was fascinated by this, which he first heard during one of his stays at the Mill House, Sidestrand, the home of 'Poppyland'. He and his friends are supposed to have frolicked over the cliffs shouting the rhyme with great joy and abandon. Several of the Mill House guests caused the locals to question the sanity of the outside world.

Many place rhymes are like Swinburne's favourite, simpy amusing alliterations and have nothing to do with the characters of their inhabitants:

> 'Holt Knowers [or Know-alls].
> Norwich Joes [or City Joes].
> Yarmouth Bloaters.
> Gorleston Jews.

Havergate Hares.
Reedham Rats,
Southwood Swine,
Cantley Cats.

Acle Asses,
Moulton Mulcs;
Beighton Bears,
And Freethorpe Fools.

Blickling Flats,
Aylsham Fliers,
Martham Peewits,
Hevingham Liars.

'Holt Knowers' comes from one of the old Gotham (town of fools) tales. The wise men of Holt having caught an owl, placed it in the waterspout of the church tower, thinking it would be drowned in the next rain. They were amazed when they saw it fly out at the top! 'Gorleston Jews' comes from a story that one of the natives, a master mariner, threw a Jew overboard in order to steal his goods.

Why your purse should come to grief at Homersfield remains a mystery:

'Denton in the Dale,
And Aldborough in the Dirt;
And if you go to Homersfield,
Your purse will get a squirt.'

The next piece of doggerel tells us something about the Norfolk villages and towns:

'Runton Dabs.
Cromer Crabs.
Beeston Babies.
Sherringham Ladies or
Sherringham Shammocks [bad-going horses].
Bessingham Bannocks.

Weybourne Witches.
Salthouse Ditches or
Salthouse Bitches.
Cley Geese.
Blakeney Bulldogs.
Morston Dodmen [snails].
Wells Bitefingers.
Langham Fairmaids.
Stiffkey or Stewkey Blues [cockles].
Binham Bulls.
Cockthorpe Slows [blind worms].
Glandford Nobles.
Baconsthorpe Strippers.
Gresham Mites.
And the Blakeney people
Stand on the steeple,
And crack hazel-nuts
With a five-farthing beetle.'

One of the inhabitants of Wells is reported to have bitten off the finger of a drowned sailor in order to get his ring. Some of the Sheringham ladies had the reputation of being rather genteel in the heyday of 'Poppyland'. I am not aware, though, of Weybourne being prolific in witches, unless this is a swipe at the local women, as could be the case at Salthouse. Were the inhabitants of Beeston once more fecund or friendly than their neighbours? And why the Blakeney people should climb their church steeple to crack hazel-nuts with a five-farthing beetle remains a mystery!

Whatever the original reason, these innocuous nonsense verses are an important part of folk history of the county.

Treachery at
St Benedict's

ST BENEDICT'S Abbey has been a landmark on the bank of the
river Bure for almost 1,000 years. Now reduced to just the
ruins of its former gatehouse, onto which was grafted a windmill
in the 18th century, it hides a mystery within its ancient walls.

Many literal and metaphorical storms have blown over the
abbey, including attack by the Normans and, 300 years later, the
Peasants' Uprising when the abbey was stormed and its deeds and
charters destroyed.

Legend states that sometimes terrible things happen at this
lonely place when that which was once sacred returns as if by the
art of some diabolical magician. To add to its horrors it is said that
once a terrible dragon which had been terrorising the people
from the neighbouring village of Ludham ended its life alongside
the abbey.

The present abbey is thought to have been built on land
granted by King Canute in 1016 although there had been a
religious establishment standing close by for many years before
that gift. Canute granted St Benedict's his manors of Horning,
Neatishead and Ludham and other landowners followed suit,
making it one of the richest abbeys in England. By the end of the
13th century it owned property in 76 Norfolk parishes.

One of the abbey's most generous benefactors was Sir John
Fastolf of Caistor Castle. He and his wife were buried in a chapel
which they had built on the site and he was the blue-print for the
Falstaff of Shakespeare's plays.

St Benedict's-at-Holm even survived the predatory Henry VIII who in 1536, in consideration of all the abbey's assets being made over to the Crown, appointed the last of its 37 abbots Bishop of Norwich, combining the two offices. In an Act of Parliament the abbot was charged to maintain at least twelve monks to continue the tradition of worship and service. St Benedict's was therefore the only religious house in England to escape the Dissolution of the Monasteries by Henry.

To reach the site by land one has to travel over the marshes along a narrow concrete road which peters out into a cart track. It is a lonely, silent journey which sharpens the imagination on a sunless winter's day. The ruins are picturesque when bathed in sunlight but they brood as eerie as a Gothic tale when seen through a tenacious river mist. A few yards away a large oak crucifix stands tall in the middle of nowhere. It marks the spot where the high altar once stood in the main abbey, which fell a long time ago. There are no remains apart for a few stones; that is until the unspeakable happens.

It is said that over the years many people have witnessed a spectral replay of an execution which happened many centuries ago. Others have testified that before the execution the abbey materialised as if conjured from the air. The ruinous mill becomes a stone church with a large tower, from which the traitor is hanged, gurgling and wriggling at the end of his rope like a prize fish hauled from the river Bure. The marsh is filled with the cries of approbation from his fellow brethren and soldiers. A likely time to see this horrible apparition is believed to be 25th May, the anniversary of the happening.

The story goes back to the time of the Norman invasion. The monks of St Benedict's withstood attack from King William's men from some four months and could have held out for much longer had it not been for treachery. The abbey's strong walls proved impregnable, there was food to last twelve months and they put their trust in God. Unfortunately a lay-brother caretaker had aspirations which did not match his lowly rank. His pride, ambition and disloyalty were, if legend is to be believed, to turn him into one of the undead.

The enemy was about to give up its efforts to seize St Benedict's. In a last effort to gain control a messenger was dispatched waving a white flag to deliver a letter to the abbot urging him to surrender. He was given permission to enter but before meeting the great man he surreptitiously handed the caretaker a note stating that his general wished to speak with him and that a safe audience was guaranteed.

The lay-brother was flattered by this request yet puzzled as to why a high ranking soldier should wish to meet with such a junior person as himself. Much intrigued he volunteered to deliver the abbot's refusal to surrender to the general, who welcomed him most cordially. He told the caretaker that he was obviously destined for a much better career than that of a lay-brother caretaker but doubted if he would ever reach his full potential within the existing order. Now, if only he would assist his army to seize the abbey he would the very next day be promoted to abbot of St Benedict's for life. Such high office was beyond the menial's wildest dreams.

The general added that there was nothing to lose, for if the abbey held out for just one more day his soldiers would attack, with terrible results. However if this 'Abbot Elect' would open the doors to the gatehouse that very night as an act of submission, all would be spared.

Although foolish, the messenger was not totally without intelligence. Surely his brethren would gang up on him once he was found out? They would never accept him as abbot. He was not even an ordained priest. He would never survive their retribution.

The cunning general replied that by using his own rank and superiority as conqueror of the abbey, the caretaker could be assured of his acceptance as head man even if it meant killing the old abbot and any rebellious monks.

The traitor returned to St Benedict's in a turmoil of fear and excitement. He was welcomed back and praised for his bravery in delivering the message. His heart was bursting with secrecy for only he knew what the future held for himself and his brethren.

The late May sunshine turned from sunset to dusk and then melted into a night as still and dark as deceit. The caretaker's blood pounded as the bell in the tower boomed out eleven times over the shadowless marshes. The last bell was followed by three gentle taps on the massive gatehouse door. The visitors had arrived. His hands shook as he slowly pulled back the strong bolt.

In a flash the soldiers burst into the sacred fortress and set about their business.

Realising their betrayal the monks offered little resistance for blood-shed was not in their hearts. Soon all arms were put aside and a truce agreed.

The following morning the entire order was summoned to the great church. To the astonishment of all the unordained caretaker was paraded in front of the large gathering. He was anointed and then dressed in a cope and mitre. The abbot's crozier was placed in his hand whereupon the general pronounced him Abbot of St Benedict's-at-Holm for life.

The proclamation was greeted with silence. The new abbot's face which was flushed with pride soon turned to deathly white as his hands were bound behind his back once the ceremony was over. Still dressed in his robes of high office the 'Abbot for Life' was dragged off by the soldiers to meet his Maker. His cries for mercy fell on deaf ears as a noose was slipped over his head. He was hoisted up onto a makeshift gibbet which was a pole secured to the lowest window of the bell tower. The new abbot dangled in full view of everyone, a gross charade of a lay-brother, stuffed with treachery and personal gain. His predecessor was later restored to office.

According to tradition the lay-brother is destined to re-enact his death over and over as a terrible warning to others who have disloyalty and ambition in their veins.

The last monk is said to have left the site in 1545. However, tradition continues for every first Sunday in August the Bishop of Norwich, as Abbot of St Benedict's, holds a service in its ruins. This is a lovely ceremony, surrounded by the summer marshes and grazing cattle, even though the river Bure is jammed with holiday boats which throb along the abbey boundaries. Many participants come to this ancient ceremony, some travelling by boat and others over land to offer their act of worship. Thoughts of ghosts and spectral buildings must be far from their minds. It is just when you are alone and the weather is dank or the day dark that a lapwing can become a death cry.

The Burston School Strike

B URSTON is a small village lying some five miles from Diss. On the village green next to the parish church, stands a small single-storey building inscribed 'Burston Strike School,' reminder of an incident which lasted from 1914 until 1939 and gave the village an international reputation.

On 31st January 1911 Tom Higdon and his wife Annie came to the village to take up teaching posts, she as the headmistress of the village school and he as her assistant.

They had not wanted to leave their former posts at Wood Dalling council school near Fakenham, where they had been engaged in a protracted battle with the managers and had been informally asked to leave. Part of the trouble had been over the Higdon's political activity in promoting Labourers' Union branches in the area and organising agricultural labourers to take over the Wood Dalling Parish Council, which had upset the balance of power within the village.

Tom and Annie were both strong minded people and dedicated teachers. When they applied for the Burston posts they had arranged for a Wood Dalling friend to write to the rector and chairman of the Burston school managers giving him a full account of their former problems. The teachers were able to provide excellent references and the couple were well received by the managers of the Burston and Shimpling council schools.

The Rev Charles Tucker Eland, rector of Burston and chairman of the managers, was soon urging the Higdons to attend his church to set a good example to the parish children.

But the Higdons, being chapel-goers, would not agree. Otherwise they experienced no trouble with the school managers for two years. They were well respected by the pupils and their parents. They offered a wide curriculum which included astronomy, knitting and photography and was far ahead of their time, in addition to the usual subjects. The children were encouraged to better themselves and Annie brought her typewriter and sewing machine to school so the girls could learn new skills.

At that time Burston had no Labourers' Union branch and wages were lower than those of Wood Dalling, the Higdon's former workplace. The church and farmers dominated the parish council, which was perceived as doing little for the improvement of its parishioners, whose housing conditions were particularly bad. The council school was in poor condition with bad lighting, drainage and ventilation.

In March 1913 the parish council elections were to take place. Noah Sandy, a smallholder and bricklayer who was in a frustrating minority amongst the predominance of landlords and farmers who were regularly re-elected to serve, called on Tom Higdon and asked if he would offer himself for election. The teacher seized upon the challenge, perhaps without giving too much thought as to what had happened at Wood Dalling and the certain knowledge that his action would bring him yet again into conflict with the church and local farmers, two of whom were Burston school managers.

Higdon was soon busy getting sufficient labourers nominated, in addition to himself and Sandy, to take over the council. The rector was defeated, Tom Higdon came top of the poll and only one farmer managed to scrape in. From that time the rector's attitude towards the Higdons changed for the worse.

Lots of petty squabbles ensued. For example Mrs Higdon had obtained permission from the vice-chairman of the school managers to close the school during a whooping cough epidemic. The chairman, Rev Eland was holidaying abroad at the time, yet upon his return Mrs Higdon was accused of making an arbitary decision to close the school. She proved that the vice-chairman had signed the appropriate notice and entered his decision in the school log book yet was still informed 'that the Committee took a very serious view of her having closed the School without

permission, but . . . the Managers will now let the matter drop.'
She was later hauled before them for lighting the school fire which had been forbidden, being regarded as an unnecessary luxury. Mrs Higdon justified her action by saying that the central heating system was inadequate and the fire was needed to be lit on some mornings to dry the children's wet clothes. The Higdons were also reprimanded for snubbing the rector and his family in the street and for entering the managers meeting without first knocking on the door and without offering them any greeting.

After various grievances from the headmistress concerning conditions at the school, which seemed to be well founded, the managers wrote to the Norfolk Education Committee complaining about her lighting of the fire and that 'as she has so many faults to find with the place, would the Committee kindly remove her to a sphere more genial?'

The final straw came when Annie Higdon, who was a fair and compassionate woman, was accused of beating two girls who had recently come from Doctor Barnardo's Home in London to be fostered by a Burston family. The day after the girls joined the school they alleged victimisation in the playground, and that one boy in particular had indecently conducted himself in their presence. They went on to accuse Annie Higdon of brutally caning them and causing the large red weals on their backs.

The managers held an enquiry, from which Mrs Higdon was absent through ill-health. In her defence witnesses had been arranged to testify that it was the foster mother herself who had beaten the children. The Barnardo's girls confessed to Mrs Ling, the infants' teacher, that their new mother had told them to say their injuries were the work of Mrs Higdon and they were afraid to go against her. They then repeated this statement to the entire school but neither the rector nor any member of the Norfolk Education Committee would come to hear their words.

It was further proven that the so-called 'rude' boy had according to the school register been absent at the time of the alleged indecent conduct. His mother had been called to the school and witnessed her son vindicated by both girls in turn each accusing the other of fabricating the story. Upon questioning at this local enquiry one of the London girls confessed that she had witnessed these things at her former school and not at Burston.

Annie Higdon insisted upon an enquiry by the Norfolk Education Committee as a means of clearing her name. She lost and was told 'The Sub-Committee, after most carefully reviewing the whole of the evidence, advise: That it is to the interest of elementary education in the village that the Head Teacher should seek other employment, with as little delay as possibly. . . .' The Higdons were dismissed on 31st March 1914.

Most of Burston was angry at the blow dealt to their headmistress and her assistant and many were prepared to boycott the council school. On the evening of their dismissal a meeting was called on the green by one of the parents to consider the question of the school and what to do about it. All kinds of workers and their wives flocked to the meeting determined that the sentences on the popular teachers should not be implemented. They booed the rector and cheered the Higdons, who took no part in the meeting.

It was later reported in the *Norwich Mercury* that the chairman proposed the following resolution: 'That we, the people and ratepayers of Burston, and the parents of the children attending Burston School, do most emphatically protest against the high-handed action of the Education Authorities in terminating the services of Mr and Mrs Higdon at Burston School. . . . That owing to the mischievous interference with the conduct of the school in regard to the Barnardo children, we protest against their attendance at the school, and their presence in the Parish.'

What the paper did not report were the children's 'secret' chalked notices which appeared all over the villages announcing their intention to strike the following day. Their leader was Violet Potter, a senior pupil aged 13 years.

According to Tom Higdon, on 1st April 1914 Mr Ikin, assistant secretary to the Norfolk Education Committee, called at Buston schoolhouse early in the morning with cheques for himself and his wife in lieu of notice. An argument ensued, the Higdons wanting three months notice instead of money.

Later that morning the green was crowded with children being lined into a procession by Violet and her helpers. When the supply teachers arrived to replace the Higdons the determined band of pupils moved off on their march around the village, waving little red flags and carrying slogans of 'We Want Our

Teachers Back'. They marched to Violet's concertina music, jeering the rector en route.

With the weather proving suitable the Higdon's gave the striking children lessons on the green. Summonses were served on parents for keeping their children away from school but the strikers held steadfast. Funds were set up to pay the fines of parents who could not meet this commitment. When it became indisputable that the striking children were in fact being tutored on a daily basis by qualified teachers, the fines ceased.

In time a carpenter's shop was used as a makeshift school room where Mrs Higdon allowed the pupils to bake potatoes for their dinner on a small portable stove. They were later evicted from this venue and used a temporary wooden building on the green. Throughout the conflict the alternative school was visited by the schools' inspectors who remained impressed with standards of education.

Mrs Higdon was evicted from the school house, having refused to move at the behest of the authorities. A crowd of villagers helped the couple move their belongings in wheelbarrows and carts to be stored in the homes of their supporters whilst they took up lodgings at the mill. The church was boycotted by the teachers' supporters and Methodist ministers conducted strike baptisms and funerals on the green.

The Agricultural Labourers' Union and the National Union of Railwaymen backed the strikers and their help increased when it was learned that those who were supporting the Higdons were deprived of their glebe land by the vicar. Numerous Trade Unions and Co-operative Societies and members of the public, from home and abroad, subscribed to a fund to construct a purpose-made Strike School. This was to be built on a parcel of land on the green which was granted by the parish council, controlled by Tom Higdon and his supporters.

The foundation stone of the new building was laid in 1917 and the school opened in 1918 with a register of 40 pupils. It is some 36 ft by 24 ft and faced with Bath stone which bears memorial inscriptions to those who gave so generously. Along the top is engraved the proud inscription 'Burston Strike School'. The village green was the children's playground. The building was also used as a meeting place and became a 'centre of rural democracy'. The Higdons increased the children's education to embrace the meaning of trade unionism, Internationalism and Christian Socialism.

The strike lasted 25 years, until Tom Higdon's death in 1939, but the building was used as a school until the 1960s. Annie Higdon died in 1946 and the two are buried side by side in the churchyard next to the Strike School.

The little building is now a museum and children's library. Inside is a board giving the names of all the children who took part in the strike and mementos of the Higdons. An annual rally and picnic are held in Burston every September.

Fish
For to Catch

THE North Sea laps coldly over Norfolk's coastal shores and has always offered a living to those who are prepared to take on its various moods.

Before the foundation of Great Yarmouth, when the valley of the Yare was still an estuary, Norwich, now some 18 miles from the sea, was an important fishing station. Its sheriffs were obliged to pay an allowance out of each new season's herrings to the Monarch in the form of herring pies, who in return rewarded them with gifts.

Great Yarmouth was for centuries made prosperous with its herring fishing from September to December. The declining industry stopped in the mid 1960s. Its 'Free Herring Fair' was one of the most important fairs of medieval Europe.

It was a hard life working on the drifters which towed a line of 100 nets or more. In the 19th century the men's earnings were doled out at Christmas, known as 'making up time'. Their pay was proportioned to the number of fish caught and the overall price gained. When the accounts were made up at the end of the season the nett profits were divided by so many shares according to pre-arrangement. For the skipper, nine hands and a boy the sharing out went something like this:

The sum would be divided into 18 equal shares: three of these went to the vessel, three for the nets, two for the skipper, one-and-a-half to the mate, one for each of the hands and a half to the boy. At the end of a good season a man could take home perhaps £30 to £60 as his share. Compare this with the rates for landworkers — twelve shillings to 13 shillings a week earned by a teamerman and ten shillings to twelve shillings by an ordinary labourer, and the three months of dangerous work showed good return.

Every herring season witnessed the drowning of men. During a terrible gale in October 1883, 210 lives were lost and a fund for the maintenance of the widows and orphans was opened at the London Mansion House.

From the 19th century hundreds of Scottish girls were employed at the South Denes to gut and prepare the fish, for by that time the number of Scottish owned vessels outnumbered local vessels at the fishery. Until the 1830s most of the fish was smoked, mainly for export as 'red-herrings', and then two new cures became popular for the English market. The lightly smoked bloater was introduced about 1836, supposedly by a Yarmouth curer named Bishop, followed in 1845 by the kipper, a salmon cure adopted for herring by John Woodger, a Newcastle curer. From the 1890s pickled herrings had overtaken the red herrings, most of which were exported to Germany and Russia.

The First World War severely restricted the fishing industry and many drifters and their crews were requisitioned by the Navy. There was a revival after the war, but the same impositions were experienced during the Second World War, after which the fishery resumed but on a much smaller scale. By 1957 stocks had dwindled through overfishing and by the mid 1960s the industry had virtually disappeared and redundant fishing premises were taken over for the search for North Sea oil and gas. There is just one steam drifter still in existence, the *Lydia Eva*, managed by a charitable trust.

There are still individual fishermen or men working in 'sets' who manage to live from general fishing around the Norfolk coast. They work long hard hours in return for little spare money. I cannot speak for those aboard the large fishing trawlers, but the 'small-timers' are generally contented people who would not swop their lives for a crock of gold. They continue to draw upon old traditions as well as new technology.

The North Norfolk coastline was a good breeding ground for shellfish. Stiffkey was especially famous for its 'Stewkey Blues' (cockles), mussels from Blakeney to Brancaster, whelks from

Wells, crabs from Cromer. In the 19th century there was an oyster boom when natural beds were discovered off the coast. Until the beginning of the 1900s some 20 boats went oyster dredging from Brancaster Staithe.

Women were still gathering cockles at Stiffkey until the start of the Second World War, although their numbers were falling from the 1930s. They were a strong breed who took the wet and cold in their stride, raking, netting and picking up the cockles which many carried on their backs over the one and a half mile trek across the marshes. The more fortunate balanced their sacks on bicycles whilst others had a donkey to bear the load. Lots of women went barefoot with their skirts hitched up around their waists to stop the hems from dragging in the water, their bare legs mottled by the cutting wind.

Old sacks were tied around their upper bodies for warmth and protection from the water which seeped from the cockle sacks. It was easy to recognise a cockler by her bent back and prominent rear end, fashioned over the years to counterbalance her heavy sack. You could also tell by her weatherbeaten complexion, chapped hands and mottled legs. Many had a coarse turn of phrase when the occasion arose, which was often. They were indeed a special type of person who earned their money the hard way.

Cockles are still harvested from around Blakeney Cut to Brancaster, mainly by boats and nets, but the majority are commercially dredged up in the Wash.

Mussels were also once picked by hand and riddled through a sieve to separate the debris. They continue to start their commercial lives in the traditional custom of being put in 'lays' (beds) by the fishermen once the main crop is finished. The 'seed' or tiny mussels are bought from suppliers via the Wash, their lays being channels which are knee deep at low tide, staked out with corks and ropes tied to anchors. At high tide the fishermen tip the seed into the prepared lays and wait patiently for 18 months until the mussels are ready for harvesting.

There was a great whelk industry in Wells where the snail-like creatures were caught in sometimes over 200 baited pots, often worked by just two men working as a 'set'. This was no easy task with pots in lines or 'shanks' of 36 pots, the whole lot needing perhaps four miles of rope and a couple of anchors plus a marker buoy.

As the pots were hauled aboard they were emptied, the old bait removed, fresh put in and the pot stowed away until the entire shank was in. Then it was off to another spot to lay the traps.

The haul was carefully picked over for parasites and then put into nets by the bushelful to be later boiled at Wells and sent off to Southend and Blackpool or wherever the shellfish counters were popular. Supplies of whelks are getting scarce, probably due to over-fishing, and many fishermen are turning their attention to crabs which are in great demand from restaurants and public houses.

Cockles, winkles and fish used to be hawked about the countryside every Saturday night, the two former being a traditional Sunday tea. On the Blakeney to Cley road there is a small rise called Mackerels Hill. Within living memory a man would come with horse and cart between ten and eleven at night with fresh mackerel, ringing his bell and offering between 20 and 30 for sixpence or one shilling. People would flock to him however late the hour.

Samphire, which grows on the marshes and can be boiled and eaten plain or pickled in vinegar, is still gathered and sold mainly in Cromer and Sheringham. Again it used to be hawked around the streets by a man with a bell crying, 'Samphire, buy your samphire!' Traditionally the best time to harvest this plant is after Lammas Day (1st August).

If you want to know what a real old fashioned kipper tastes like you should pay a call on the Cley Smoke House at Cley Next the Sea where the fish are smoked on the premises. Once you have eaten a plump, uncoloured, juicy, wood-smoked kipper which nearly touches both sides of a dinner plate, you will be spoilt for life. The dark brown, salty, commercially produced variety bear no resemblance to the real thing.

Sea trout are in season from April to August and fishermen once did a good trade in this fish, going out at night close to shore and wading in up to the chest if a boat was not handy. Before waterproof waders were readily available they went into the water dressed in plenty of woollies for warmth. Even when wet they were said to be the best garments to wear and certainly preferable to bathing shorts and a bare chest.

A livelihood from the sea has never been easy and in the old days there was extreme poverty when the men could not cast off for perhaps a week or even a month in really bad weather. They relied on the kindness of local shop keepers to give them 'tick' or credit until they got back to work. This rarely proved to be a problem within a small community, each knowing the other and certain that the sea would yield in its own good time.

It was once customary for many fishermen to say a prayer before casting off and one found in a book of Norfolk customs published in 1885 is as follows:

'Pray God lead us,
Pray God speed us,
From all evil defend us.
Fish for our pains God send us,
Well to fish and haul,
And what He pleases to pay us all,
A fine night to land our nets,
And safe in with the land —
Pray God, hear my prayer.'

Coastal fishing remains an entire way of life for the small sets of fishermen who know and respect the fickle ways of the elements. The sea has burnished and furrowed their faces. Even age has trouble harnessing a true fisherman, the call of the sea is too strong.

The
Treasure of
Callow Pit

THERE is a traditional tale connected with Southwood, a small village between Yarmouth and Norwich, concerning golden treasure which lies at the bottom of 'Callow Pit'. This is an ancient cavernous pit which lies on the boundary of Southwood and Moulton. At the end of the 19th century a folklorist collected the tale from a local clergyman, who obtained the account from a middle-aged woman, one of the 39 inhabitants of the parish.

The pit was then in a remote part of the village and had long been avoided by people at night for it was reported that a headless horseman frequently rode past that spot. In the past the pit had been used by smugglers for hiding their contraband.

The woman recounted the popular tale of a large quantity of gold locked in an iron chest that lay submerged in the bottom of Callow Pit, for although now dry and thoroughly searched for treasure it was once deep with water.

Once upon time two daring men who firmly believed in the legend determined to search for the chest. Keeping their plans secret they waited patiently until the waters were at their lowest. They placed their ladders across the pit to form a bridge and worked their way to the middle. By means of a strong staff with an iron hook they fished around in the murky water and eventually caught hold of the ring in the lid of the chest. With great effort the chest was raised onto the temporary bridge. It was decided that the best way to carry their find was to put the staff through the ring, thus bearing the weight of the heavy treasure trove on their shoulders.

The narrator continued that, whether dealing with demons or fairies, the popular belief is that silence is essential to success and in this case one of the men was so excited by their tremendous find that he cried out, 'We've got it safe, and Old Nick himself can't get it from us!'

The pit was instantly enveloped by a dense sulphuric-smelling vapour and a black hand and arm said to belong to Satan, was thrust up through the water and seized the coveted chest. A desperate struggle ensued between the three, the chest separated from the ring and returned to its original home never to be seen again. The ring remained on the staff and the disappointed men decided to fix the proof of their adventure to the door of Southwood church which is now a ruin. The ring has now been transferred to the door of nearby Limpenhoe church.

Nelson,
Hero of Norfolk

Horatio Nelson, hero of the Nile, Copenhagen and Trafalgar, was born on 29th September 1758 at the rectory, Burnham Thorpe where his father was the incumbent. Nelson's birthplace has long since gone and is replaced by the present rectory. There is a local legend that the great man was not born at the vicarage at all, but in the large flint barn next to the village public house, Mrs Nelson having gone into rapid labour whilst out on a drive and not being able to make the vicarage in time.

During the same year as his birth the Admiralty placed an order with the Chatham dockyard for a ship which when launched in 1765 was named the *Victory*, and was to become as famous as Vice-Admiral, Viscount Nelson.

Horatio was the sixth of eleven children and was such a weakling that it was doubted if he would survive for long. He was dogged by ill health throughout his life and only stood at five ft six inches in his stockinged feet, but his spirit was mightier than his frail body.

His father, rector of All Saints' church, Burnham Thorpe, for 46 years, was a strong disciplinarian who 'deemed it an indulgence for a back to touch the back of a chair' at table. Nelson's mother, Catherine Suckling, was born in the rectory at Beccles, Suffolk, and on 11th May 1749 she was married at St Michael's church, Beccles to the Rev Edmund Nelson, who had been curate at Beccles from 1745 to 1747. She died when Horatio was nine years old.

Brooks and rivers attracted the young boy and he loved to play by the little river that originates at South Creake and flows out to Burnham at Overy Staithe. The North Sea was only a few miles from his home and when storms raged sea gulls would take shelter in the rectory garden. It is a popular belief in Norfolk that sea gulls are dead mariners reincarnate. The frail child with a chronic nasal problem which caused him to always 'speak through his nose', who fed bread to the visitors from the angry sea, was destined to become England's finest mariner.

At the age of nine he attended Norwich grammar school. This was followed by a spell at Downham Market school and then to Paston grammar school at North Walsham. On its roof is a cut-out HMS *Victory* weathervane and one of the school houses is named after their famous pupil. The school was run on strong disciplinarian lines which helped form young Horatio's character but did not dampen his spirit. When he was caught scrumping pears by night from the headmaster's garden he is said to have replied, 'I only took them because every other boy was afraid.'

When Mrs Nelson died in 1767 her brother Captain Maurice Suckling offered to take one of his brother-in-law's children and Horatio was chosen. At the age of twelve he happened to read in the *Norwich Mercury* that Captain Suckling had been appointed to the 64-gun *Raisonnable*. The news excited the young lad who wrote immediately to one of his brothers to ask their father, who was convalescing from illness at Bath, if he might join his uncle's ship.

Edmund Nelson agreed but Captain Suckling's reply was not encouraging. He not only expressed his surprise that such a puny boy should want to go to sea but considered that a cannon-ball would probably knock off his head in his first battle, which would quickly settle the matter. Suckling made it perfectly clear to his brother-in-law that the thought of making a sailor out of Nelson was ridiculous, but one cold morning the call came to Paston grammar school for the boy to make haste to his uncle's ship which was lying in the Medway. At that time life at sea was exceptionally harsh, when floggings, drunkenness, mutiny and even killing were commonplace.

On 1st January 1771 he joined *Raissonnable* as 'captain's servant' but shortly the whole crew was paid off, including

Nelson. Soon Suckling got command of another ship — *Triumph* — and his nephew joined him. Later he was sent on a merchant ship to the West Indies to be taught some practical seamanship and on his return Nelson joined the *Carcass* on an expedition to the Arctic.

One night when the ship was jammed in pack ice, Nelson and a shipmate climbed overboard in the hope of shooting a polar bear. Nelson wanted its skin as a souvenir for his father. The gun locked tight but Nelson ran towards the ferocious creature wanting to club it with his useless musket. The crew, fearing for the life of the young man, fired a shot from the ship and the frightened bear ran off. The captain of the *Carcass*, Admiral Lutwidge, regularly dined off this story once his young seaman had become famous.

Inspired for adventure after the Arctic expedition he was next appointed to the frigate *Seahorse*, bound for the East Indies, but after two years and consequent bad health was invalided home with the threat of having to give up a career at sea.

However his strong spirit triumphed and he announced, 'Well then, I will be a hero, and confiding in Providence, I will brave every danger.'

In 1777 he was made a lieutenant and joined the 32-gun frigate *Lowestoft*, was promoted to commander in 1778 and took charge of a brig called *Badger*. He was further promoted in 1779 to captain and after a spell of service in the West Indies was back home again with fever.

The Nelson determination soon had him back at sea and in 1782 at Quebec he experienced the first of his many love affairs, for despite his thin short body and nasal voice twinged with a Norfolk accent he was quite a ladies man.

In 1784 he was back in the West Indies where he met and married Frances Herbert Nisbet, a 26 year old widow with a five year old son. They returned to England where Nelson remained for five years without work and on half-pay. Their impecunious state forced them to live at Burnham Thorpe rectory.

It is said he was quite a danger at the many shooting parties which set off from Burnham Thorpe by the way in which he carried his gun 'always cocked, as if he were going to board an enemy, and his custom of firing immediately when any birds appeared, rendered any attendance on him a service a considerable danger.'

He was rescued from the life of a 'land lubber' in 1793 when war broke out with France. He was given the 64-gunned *Agamemnon* which was to become his best liked ship. The Admiralty agreed to his request that they should defer posting bills in London advertising for crew for the ship. Nelson knew the worth of his fellow Norfolkmen who were responding to the bills already displayed in his home county, where a lieutenant and four midshipmen were collecting a 'stiffening of Norfolk volunteers — worth two of other men.' Throughout his naval career he always applied for crew at East Anglian ports. Before he took command of the *Agamemnon* Nelson held a dinner at a local public house, now name the Lord Nelson, for all the Burnham villagers.

Nelson lost the sight of his right eye in 1794 at Calvi in Corsica and as a rear-admiral in 1797 he made an unsuccessful night-attack on Santa Cruz, Tenerife which resulted in the amputation of his right arm. The surgeon botched the operation and Nelson always referred to the stump as his 'fin'.

On 1st August 1798 he fought the first of his three great battles — the Battle of the Nile, and for this great victory was made Baron Nelson of the Nile and, 'every court in Europe bestowed awards and decorations upon him'.

Later that year in Naples he renewed his friendship with Emma Hamilton whom he had first met in 1793. A flotilla of boats including one with Sir William Hamilton, the British Ambassador and his wife Lady Hamilton on board, came out to meet his battered ship to the playing of Rule Britannia.

Emma Hamilton started life as a servant girl. After being seduced and abandoned by a naval officer she became the mistress of Charles Greville, son of Lord Warwick, who subsequently sold her to his uncle, Sir William Hamilton who treated her well and eventually married her. Her subsequent love affair with Horatio Nelson was to shock the nation.

The Nelson whom Lady Hamilton met at Naples was quite different to the· dashing young man she had met five years previously. Instead she was confronted with 'a feeble, pale wreck, one eye blinded, one arm hacked off, a fresh wound healing on his forehead: a man aged and worn by the stress of grim fighting.' She is said to have fainted at the sight of him and his injuries made her love him.

Nelson had seen very little of Frances during their ten years of married life and it has been suggested that he never really loved her. However in January 1789 he purchased Roundwood Place, Victory Road, Ipswich, as a home for his wife and father who lived there until 1800. In 1801 Nelson settled half his income on Fanny and insisted that they become permanently separated.

Also in that year, Lady Hamilton bore Nelson a daughter, Horatia. At the time of the birth Nelson settled Emma and Sir William Hamilton, who was to live for two more years, in a house at Merton Place, Surrey. The first Earl of Minto, Sir Gilbert Elliot wrote an account of their lives:

'I went to Lord Nelson's on Saturday to dinner . . . and she and Sir William and the whole set of them are living with him at his expense. She is in high looks but more immense than ever. . . . The love she makes to him (Nelson) is not only ridiculous but disgusting. Not only the rooms, but the whole house, staircase and all, are covered with nothing but pictures of her and him, of all sizes and sorts. . . .'

For some time the illegitimate birth was kept a careful secret between the two lovers and in correspondence they pretended the child had other parents. The father, 'Mr Thompson' was supposed to be a young officer serving with Nelson while Emma pretended to be looking after 'Mrs Thompson' and the baby. Nelson could therefore be kept up to date with news without giving the game away.

Given command in the Baltic he was responsible for the victory at Copenhagen in 1801 and was created viscount upon his return to England. In 1803 he became commander in the Mediterranean where he blockaded Toulon for 18 months, but in 1805 the French escaped with Nelson in hot pursuit, the chase culminating in the battle of Trafalgar.

On 21st October 1805, the day on which he died, Nelson drew up his famous memorandum which he called 'The Nelson Touch' containing his plan of action for the ensuing conflict. As the two British lines led by Nelson and Collingwood sailed into battle the Norfolk hero delivered the signal: 'England expects that every man will do his duty.' Then with the two great fleets approaching each other he entered in his diary '. . . And may no misconduct in any one tarnish it: And may humanity after victory be the predominant feature in the British fleet. . . .'

'The Nelson Touch' worked with 20 enemy ships captured or sunk and some 12,000 prisoners taken. All this achieved with 27 ships against the enemy's 33.

But England paid its price, not only in its dead and wounded sailors, but the loss of its greatest seaman of all time, Vice-Admiral Horatio, Viscount Nelson. *Victory* collided with the enemy *Redoubtable* and with their riggings entwined the crews fought muzzle to muzzle. After 30 minutes of fierce fighting Nelson was shot through the spine by a French sniper.

As Nelson, aged 47 years, lay dying, a surgeon at his side, Captain Hardy, informed him that 15 enemy ships had struck their colours.

'That is well', he said, 'But I bargained for 20. . . . Don't throw me overboard, Hardy. Take care of poor Lady Hamilton, Hardy: never forget Horatia. Kiss me, Hardy.'

He died at 4.30 pm soon after uttering the words, 'God and my country'.

Nelson's body was returned to England and on 9th January 1806 he received a state funeral and was buried at St Paul's Cathedral. Six admirals carried his coffin to its final resting place. Seven dukes, another 25 admirals and a hundred captains in full dress were amongst the mourners.

Great Yarmouth later commemorated its county's hero by building the Nelson Column on the South Denes, the first stone being laid on 15th August 1817. It originally stood alone but over the years has been surrounded by industrial development. The whole structure is 144 ft high with a small viewing platform at the top, between the caryatids which support a cupola surrounded by the figure of Britannia. Britannia faces inland towards the harbour.

A caretaker whose duties included collecting admission money to the viewing platform, lived in a cottage built to the south of the column. The first post holder was James Sharman, who was born in Yarmouth in 1785 and at the age of 14, whilst working at the Wrestlers inn close to St Nicholas' church, was press ganged into the Navy. He joined *Victory* and was said to have helped carry the fatally wounded Nelson to his cabin. After a long service he was discharged from the Navy and became the keeper of the monument on the recommendation of Captain Hardy of *Victory* fame.

Later, Charles Dickens, who was holidaying at Great Yarmouth, visited Sharman and is said to have modelled the character of Ham Peggotty in *David Copperfield* on this 'old salt'.

There are various pieces of Nelson memorabilia at Nelson Hall and the parish church at Burnham Thorpe. A replica of the flag that he flew as Commander-in-Chief at the Battle of the Nile is flown from the church on special feast days.

'Giles Jolterhead and his Darter Dinah'

SAMUEL Lane was born in the parish of St Gregory, Norwich, in 1786. He was a brilliant writer of ballads and poetry and all his material dealt with local topics. When he was a boy he suffered a terrible injury and was disabled for life. He was frequently out of work and often in debt. When the need arose he earned some money by writing and the more he drank the more he wrote, so he wrote a lot of ballads and was usually drunk! He spent some time in the workhouse, but the persistently offensive verses which he wrote on the walls concerning the governors got him thrown out. He was such a popular writer that his ballads sold in their thousands.

The following entitled *The Dialogue between Giles Jolterhead and his Darter Dinah on their visit to the Norwich Festival* is considered to be his best.

> 'Giles Jolterhead! from Ashwellthorpe, a joskin raw was he,
> To Norwich came on Tuesday last, our Festival to see;
> "Consarne my carcase," now says Giles,
> "I'll take my eldest darter,
> And to the Festival we'll go, and see what they are arter.

Come Dinah, mor, put on your duds, and make yourself
    look tidy,
Who knows amongst there lords and dukes what good luck
    may betide ye;
For dukes, and lords, and noblemen, in spite of all their
    bother,
Will sometimes fall in love, they say, with a red raw country
    mawther."

Then off to Norwich arm in arm, they smash'd along right
    well,
And when they got to town set up at the Barking Dicky
    Hotel,
On rolls and cheese, and decent swipes, so comfortably they
    baited,
Till Giles declared he felt himselt more than half way
    "coxelated".

Giles paid his reckoning like a man, and off they both did
    toddle,
But where to find the Festival, put both of them in a
    muddle;
They enquired of everybody they met "where the Festival
    was held?"
Some said on "Heigham Cawnser" and some in "Chapel
    Field".

Some said t'was held on the Ditches, at the Holkham Arms
    or Chequers,
Whilst others swore right hard and fast 'twas held at the Nut
    Crackers.
At last they saw some carriages a smashing might and main,
So Giles and Dinah ran behind till they got to St Andrew's
    Plain.

"Consarne it, Dinah, mor" says Giles, "here's a bustle and
    confusion,
Do they call this a Festival? Why 'tis more like a Revolution.
Here's the horse soldiers with their broad swords drawn up
    in battle array,
If the people do not mind their work, they'll surely kill and
    slay.

"By gums," says Giles, "now Dinah, mor, the safest way I
    think,
As we are no Revolutioners, is to climb St Andrew's Bank."
"No, no," says Dinah, "that won't do, to the Festival we are
    come,
And to see it I am determined before I do go home."

Then away they crush'd through thick and thin, in spite of
    war's alarms;
Giles flourished high his crab stick with Dinah under his
    arm;
The gentry pouring in the Hall, Giles thought he needs
    must follow,
Till a consequential door keeper cry'd "Stop! you country
    fellow."

"What for," quoth Giles, "you saucy scamp, I'll get the King
    to fine ye,
My name it is Giles Jolterhead, and this is my mawther
    Dinah;
We are all the way from Ashwellthorpe, this Festival to see,
Besides my mawther have a mind a lady for to be."

Then up there came a great stout man, with a rare large
    three-cocked squiver,
With a great red nose on his fat face, like a lump of bullock's
    liver.
"Lawk! who is he," says Dinah, "he looks for full of wrath?"
"Why that," says Giles, "'tis my belief, is his Majesty William
    the Fourth."

And with that Giles made a reverend bow, and sung God
    save the King,
The constable catch'd him a box on the ear, which made his
    thick head ring.
"Come dash my buttons though," says Giles, "it that is the
    way you treat me,
If ever I come to a Festival again, I'll give you leave to beat
    me."

Then next there comes the bellman, with his plate on his left
    breast,
Says Giles, "That's the Duke of Sussex, or else my mark I
    have missed;
If I could but speak to his Grace I wouldn't mind laying a
    penny,
That if his Highness be not engaged, he would marry my
    mawther Dinah."

But his Highness pass'd with a lofty air, and took no notice
    of Giles,
Nor did he deign to cast one look on Dinah's amorous
    smiles.
"Consarne these dukes and lords," quoth Giles, "what a set
    of chaps they are,
They certainly don't like Dinah, because she have got sandy
    hair."

And then came a lady all in white with rings on her fingers
    three,
Says Giles, "Look, Dinah, that's the Queen, God save her
    majesty;
I have a good mind to step up to her Grace, and say that I
    waited upon her,
To ask if she can't give Dinah a place as one of her maids of
    honour."

But the lady frowned, as well she might, at Giles's red-raw
    fist,
She took his nose betwixt her fingers, and gave it a
    lime-burner's twist.
"Consarne it," says Giles, "leave go of my snout or you'll
    spoil my constitution;
By George, if you treat you subjects so, no wonder at this
    revolution."

And now the fiddles began for to squeak, the trumpets, and
    the bassoons;
Says Giles, "The rebellion is broke out in the hall and these
    are the dying groans;
Run, Dinah! run, mor!" now quoth Giles, "before their
    bayonets prick ye."
Then off they quickly ran away to their quarters at the
    Barking Dickey,'

NOTE: Explanation of some dialect words:
Mawther — young girl
Joskin raw — country bumpkin
Mor — mine
Duds — best clothes
Barking Dicky Hotel — Barking Donkey Hotel
Decent swipes — good food
Coxelated — drunk
Baited — ate

The
Sword and Oak
of Winfarthing

I T was a sad day in 1949 for the small village of Winfarthing near
Diss when its mighty but almost dead oak tree, known as the
Winfarthing Oak, was dashed to the ground during a storm.

It had stood for over 1,600 years on land now belonging to
Lodge Farm. Another large tree called the Companion Oak once
stood close by but toppled sometime around the turn of the 19th
century.

The Winfarthing Oak, which within memory was heavily
swathed in iron bands and wooden support props, had been
standing when the royal manor of Winfarthing, which included a
deer park, was given to Sir William Montchesny by King Harold,
allowing the beneficiary and his heirs the right, "To hunt hare,
fox and rare wild cat' here forever.

In 1800 the proud tree measured 40 ft round the trunk and 70
ft around its base. A box was placed beside it to receive
contributions from the many visitors who came to see this
magnificent specimen, all donations going to the Foreign Bible
Service. The box was inscribed:

'Ye who this venerable oak survey,
Which still survives through many a stormy day,
Deposit here your mite with willing hands,
To spread in foreign climes, through foreign lands,
The sacred volume, so divinely given
Whose pages lead to harrow way to Heaven.'

THE SWORD AND OAK OF WINFARTHING

A member of the Cole family upon whose land the oak tree stood remembers playing in the hollow tree when he was young. He could climb right to the top from inside its massive trunk. Farm animals took shelter in its hollow and one old ivy-clad prop had rotted away to be replaced by the roots of the ivy, which did a good job. When the valiant tree blew down it was sawn up and burned. Some of the good pieces were turned into family mementos including inscribed spill holders and ash trays.

Happily descendants of the Winfarthing Oak are thriving. A local family who emigrated to Canada took some of its acorns and planted an avenue of oaks in Toronto, called the 'Winfarthing Avenue'. The acorn buried in the village green by an old lady many years past is flourishing.

The village has another piece of interesting history, this time centred around its parish church. At the east end of the south aisle of St Mary's there was formerly the chapel of the Good Sword of Winfarthing.

It is said that a sword was left in the church by a robber who had taken sanctuary within its walls and afterwards escaped. Upon its discovery it was named the Sword of the Good Thief and was considered a precious relic. There were 'offerings, vow makings, kissing and crouching' made by the numerous pilgrims who came to Winfarthing to offer prayers and gifts to this revered weapon.

Although long since vanished, its reputed existence forms part of Norfolk's folklore. The sword, which was claimed to be especially good for finding lost things and in particular strayed horses, also had additional powers useful to disgruntled and unhappy wives.

If a woman burned a candle beneath the Sword of the Good Robber every Sunday for a year she would obtain release from her husband by shortening his life. 'Her light was his extinguisher'.

According to a cutting pasted in St Mary's visitors information book this sword was first considered to be miraculous after a sad woman desperate to have a child handled the sword out of curiosity and not long afterwards became pregnant. 'Then were the monks fain to believe what the grateful criminal had told them.' A shrine was built to which people came from far and near with their prayers and gifts.

107

The same source of information makes no mention of the popular and well documented belief concerning disenchanted wives which also appears elsewhere in the scrapbook. A different version is told whereby if a candle was burned for a year before the shrine a husband's affection could be retained or returned. This would be the opposite of its popular acclaim.

In addition it suggests romantic properties, for any youth who came barefoot and 'made long and humble supplication then would his lady be like to look on him with favour,' even if she had previously rejected him. Devout couples could present themselves before its glistening blade to ensure a fruitful marriage.

The legend of the oak and the sword are depicted in the Cole memorial window which was dedicated in 1957. Lying in the shadow at the foot of the oak is a deer — a reminder that once Winfarthing was part of a Royal Deer Park. A kneeling figure holding a sword represents the legend of the 'Good Sword of Winfarthing'. Below these figures is an old plough, symbolic of local agriculture and also of ploughing matches which featured in the life of the village.

The
Swaffham Pedlar

THE parish church of Swaffham, dedicated to St Peter and St Paul, is one of the finest of the many medieval churches in East Anglia. It was built for the most part between 1454–1490 on the remains of the previous church which had partly collapsed.

According to tradition its rebuilding and restoration was in the main due to the generosity of a humble Swaffham pedlar named John Chapman. He was a good and philanthropic man, but at one time so poor he could barely keep body and soul together, that is until he dreamed his extraordinary dream.

On three successive nights he was told in his sleep that he should go to London Bridge where he would hear something to his advantage. He could not wash the dreams from his memory and received no rest from the nagging in his brain, over and over came the command, he had to go to London.

Eventually with just his dog for a companion he set off on the long and difficult walk to the capital. At last he reached his destination and stood on the bridge for several hours, feeling rather silly for having come on such a wild goose chase for what appeared to be nothing.

Just as he was about to leave for home a shopkeeper asked the pedlar what he was doing loitering on the bridge for so long. Chapman replied, without giving his name or whereabouts, that he had indeed come upon a very foolish errand and repeated his dream to the stranger.

The shopkeeper laughed and replied that if he gave in to dreams he would have set off for Swaffham in Norfolk some time

ago as he had dreamed that in that town there lived a pedlar by the name of John Chapman who had a pot of treasure buried under a tree in his garden. He added that if he believed in such nonsense he would have dug around the tree and been a rich man by now.

Chapman's face did not change expression but bidding the tradesman good day he quickly gathered up his dog and set off at a brisk pace for his home town.

To his delight everything was as foretold for after much digging he found a large pot crammed with gold coins, which he cunningly hid amongst his other brass pots for safety, keeping the contents undisturbed.

Some months later a man of learning called at his house and whilst looking at the goods on display noticed the treasure pot, which bore a Latin inscription whose meaning was unknown to the pedlar. He translated this for Chapman as 'Under me doth lie another much richer than I.' The clever pedlar merely said that when he bought the pot it was standing on top of another which was twice as big. However under cover of night he went to his special tree and dug much deeper, unearthing another pot both twice as large and full as the first which he likewise added to his stock.

Time passed yet he did not reveal his wealth, living as simply as always like a common hardworking pedlar, walking long distances hawking his wares from door to door.

For many years the parish church had been in need of repair and restoration. As there were insufficient funds for this purpose it was at last decided to impose a tax upon the townsfolk to implement the essential work, if they were not to lose their place of worship.

The pedlar knew that his moment had arrived and, having determined the cost of work needed to provide a new north aisle and tall tower steeple, Chapman agreed to bear it all without divulging the source of his wealth.

The 19th century furniture in the church has some medieval wood carvings incorporated in the clergy stalls. On the south stall are two effigies of a man with a pack on his back under which is a chained and muzzled dog. On the north stall are two of a shopkeeper under which is a carving of a woman said to be the pedlar's wife, who is looking over a shop door, each carving showing a rosary. These were taken from the family pews of John Chapman, benefactor and churchwarden of the church during its building (1462).

The two front facing chancel pews also have fine carvings at either end, one of a man carrying a pack and on the other that of a chained and muzzled dog.

There is no doubt that John Chapman, pedlar or merchant of Swaffham, was a real person and a successful businessman who used his wealth to help his church.

The
Babes in The Wood

WAYLAND or Wailing Wood is an ancient woodland lying close to Watton, near Thetford. Since medieval times it has provided a continual supply of poles from such species as bird cherry. Its hazel is used for fuel, hurdles, thatching spars and broomhandles. The larger trees provided materials for ships, barns and houses.

There is another side to this lovely old wood. For many centuries it has been associated with the broadside ballad *The Children in the Wood or The Norfolk Gentleman's Last Will and Testament*, known better to us as the nursery tale and pantomime story 'The Babes in the Wood'.

The original ballad was published in chapbook form; probably the first was in 1595 by Thomas Millington of Norwich. Other publishing houses soon brought out varying versions of the tale and these little books were hawked by street traders or chapmen. The sentiments as portrayed in these early chapbooks formed the basis of many Victorian novelettes and 'penny dreadfuls'.

The Babes in the Wood tales generally tell of the sad fate of two very young children often called Edgar and Jane Truelove, the children of Arthur Truelove, Norfolk gentleman who at the beginning of the tale is lying beside his wife both 'sore sick and like to die'. The children's downfall is brought about by the greed of their 'wicked uncle' and two local ruffians Rawbones and Woldkill. The first ballad was extremely popular and has been described as, 'One of the darling songs of the common people and the delight of most Englishmen in some part of their age.' Some of its verses are used in the following tale:

'Now ponder well, you parents dear,
These words, which I shall write;
A doleful story you shall hear,
In time brought forth to light.
A gentleman of good account
In Norfolk dwelt of late,
Who did in honour far surmount
Most men of his estate.

Sore sick was he, and like to die
No help his life could save;
His wife by him as sick did lie,
And both possessed one grave,
No love between these two was lost,
Each was to other kind,
In love they liv'd, in love they died,
And left two babes behind.'

The two dying parents had left provision in their wills for a paternal uncle to look after their orphans, the eldest being Edgar, aged three, and the younger Jane. The boy was to inherit £300 a year upon coming of age, the girl was to received £500 upon marriage. Should they both predecease their uncle without issue he was to inherit his brother's wealthy estate.

The 'wicked uncle' had no regard whatsoever for his charges but his wife adored them. By the end of the first year his indifference towards the babes grew into hatred. His brother's fortune was too dazzling a prize which only their death could procure.

He hired two villains to do the deed, having told his wife that the children would be better cared for by friends in London. They made a happy crew as they set off on horseback, not to the City but to Wayland Woods where the dirty deed was to be done.

'Away then went those pretty babes,
Rejoycing at that tide,
Rejoycing with a merry mind,
That should on cock-horse ride.
They prate and prattle pleasantly,
As they rode on the way
To those that should their butchers be
And work their lives decay.'

The children were so lovable that they melted the hearts of
their assassins, who by now were wishing they had never struck
such a financially rewarding but otherwise terrible bargain with
the Norfolk gentleman. One refused to proceed with the act, the
other said they must. Their argument turned into a fight ending
in the death of the less compassionate villain. The other led the
children deeper and deeper into the gloomy wood, telling them
to stay there until he returned with food, for by now the little ones
were ravenous.

'The pretty babes, with hand in hand,
Went wandering up and down;
But never more could see the man
Approaching from the town;
Their pretty lips with blackberries,
Were all besmear'd and dyed
And when they saw the darksome night,
They sat them down and cryed.

Thus wandered these poor innocents,
Till death did end their grief
In one another's arms they died
As wanting due relief;
No burial this pretty pair
Of any man receives,
Till Robin-redbreast piously
Did cover them with leaves.'

The uncle in the ballad soon received his come-uppance. His
house was robbed, his barns burned to the ground, his cattle died

and his two sons drowned at sea. Within seven years he had been forced to mortgage all his possessions, spent time in gaol and died owing a considerable fortune.

As to the fate of the remaining assassin:

'The fellow, that did take in hand
These children for to kill
Was for a robbery judg'd to die
Such was God's blessed will;
Who did confess the very truth,
As here hath been display'd:
Their uncle having died in gaol,
Where he for debt was laid.

You that executors be made,
And overseers eke,
Of children that be fatherless,
And infants mild and meek,
Take you example by this thing,
And yield to each his right,
Lest God with such like misery
Your wicked minds requite.'

The ballad is reputed to centre around an incident in the de Grey family of Griston Hall, Norfolk.

In 1562 the father of seven year old Thomas de Grey died, leaving the child a ward of Queen Elizabeth. Thomas was married in infancy to Elizabeth Drury and then returned to Norfolk where he was to inherit his father's considerable estate upon reaching the age of majority. The child's uncle, brother of the deceased Robert de Grey, was to inherit everything should the child die without leaving issue.

Uncle Robert was an unpopular Catholic dissenter or 'Popish Recusant' and much hated by the local Protestant folk on this account and he showed little regard for Thomas.

Four years after his father's death the child went to stay with his step-mother, Temperance Carewe, being his father's second wife, who by this time was remarried to Sir Christopher Heydon of Baconsthorpe, a Protestant. It was whilst staying at his mother's house that Thomas died in mysterious circumstances and the anti-Catholic feeling which prevailed in the area led to rumours that Robert de Grey had lent a hand in the affair. Gossip was further fuelled by the quick time in which he claimed his inheritance.

Like the villainous uncle in the ballad, he came to no good. As a recusant he was first gaoled at Norwich and then London and on his death the sum of £1,780 was owed to the Crown in respect of unpaid fines. The villain's two sons were drowned on a journey to Portugal and his later years were spent in misery.

In 1879 a huge oak tree was destroyed by lightning in Wayland Wood. Its trunk at five ft from the ground was said to measure twelve ft in circumference. Traditionally this was believed to have been the very tree under which the babes died in Wailing Wood, so called because the sound of the wind in the trees was really the pitiful ghostly cries of the little children who had once called for help in vain.

Our Lady
of Walsingham

S INCE the first shrine of Our Lady of Walsingham was founded
at Little Walsingham over 900 years ago, this market town
which lies in the valley of the river Stiffkey has been the
destination of countless pilgrims. It is also known as 'England's
Nazareth', brought about by a dream in the reign of King Edward
the Confessor.

In 1061 the Lady Richeldis de Faverche, widow of the lord of
the manor of Walsingham, had a dream in which the Blessed
Virgin Mary instructed her to have built a replica of the Holy
House of Nazareth where Mary was told by the Archangel
Gabriel that she was to bear the Son of God. Legend states that the
original Nazarene dwelling had been miraculously transported
by angels to the Sancta Casa at Loretto. Lady Richeldis was told
the site would be revealed by the sprouting of a fresh spring of
water.

The spring gushed forth and a simple shrine was built over it.
However the building was continuously disturbed for no
accountable reason. Lady Richeldis spent one entire night in
prayer and the next morning the little house had been moved as if
by God's hand to the site of twin wells some 200 ft west of the
original site.

One day the statue of Our Lady of Walsingham miraculously
appeared in the shrine, where it remained until Henry VIII
sacked the place at the time of the Dissolution and had the effigy
burned at Chelsea, London.

Many favours were granted at Little Walsingham and

thousands of pilgrims travelled to the place by land and sea, as is still the custom. Their number was so great that the road to the Holy House became one of the main highways in England.

Those pilgrims who came from the North passed through Lynn, which offered them a chapel, and they then passed on to the priories of Flitcham and Coxford. Another great road led from Yarmouth, through Norwich and Attleborough, past the hospital of Bec where 13 beds for Walsingham pilgrims were ready every night. At South Acre, West Acre, Hilborough, Prior's Thorns, Stanhoe, Caston and other places as well as Lynn, special chapels were provided for the wayside devotions of the holy travellers. The cluster of stars known as the Milky Way became popularly known as the 'Walsingham Way', as it was popularly believed to point to England's Nazareth, whose myriad roads likewise resembled this galaxy.

In 1153 a priory of Augustinian canons was formed to care for the shrine and the tiny little hamlet grew into a sizeable market town with many shops to cater for the pilgrims' needs.

For centuries the shrine was the largest place of pilgrimage throughout England, surpassing even Canterbury. Most kings of England from Henry III to Henry VIII made pilgrimages to Little Walsingham, the latter walking barefoot for the last part of the journey. There is a 14th century Slipper Chapel in the neighbouring parish of Houghton St Giles once used by the pilgrims to Walsingham to leave their shoes and walk the last mile barefoot.

When Katherine of Aragon wrote to the king announcing the victory of Flodden (1513) she concluded: 'and now go to Our Lady of Walsingham, that I promised soo long agoo to see.' In her will Katherine, who died in january 1536, provided that some personage should go to Our Lady of Walsingham on pilgrimage, distributing 20 nobles (gold coins) on the way.

One of the most precious relics which the monastery possessed was the 'Sacred Milk'. Desiderius Erasmus (1466–1536) the Dutch Christian humanist and writer, visited the shrine from Cambridge in 1511. He wrote that the substance was said to be the 'heavenly milk of the Blessed Virgin' and was stored in a crystal ampoule which was kissed by the kneeling pilgrims.

He was then shown an enormous finger joint supposed to be

that of St Peter. 'Then', exclaimed Erasmus, 'St Peter must have been a man of prodigious stature!' at which one of the pilgrims unfortunately laughed and the guide was only to be appeased by the payment of an extra fee.

Despite Henry VIII's many pilgrimages to the Norfolk shrine and priory they were stripped of everything after the Dissolution. In June 1538 Bishop Latimer wrote to Thomas Cromwell, second Minister to Henry VIII, suggesting the burning of the image of the virgin of Walsingham and others: 'They would make a joly mustere in Smythfeld.' A further letter was written on 18th June 1538, 'This day our late lady of Walsingham was brought to Lambithe, where was both my Lord Chancellor and my Lord Privy Seal with many virtuous prelates, but there was offered neither oblation nor candle. What shall become of her is not determined.' Later the statue was burned at Chelsea.

Notwithstanding the destruction of the priory and its adjuncts and the execution of its sub-prior it was found impossible to eradicate at once the belief in the minds of people in the virtues of Our Lady of Walsingham.

In 1564 Thomas Cromwell received a report of 'a poor woman of Wells, who imagined a false tale of a miracle done by the image of Our Lady after it had been carried away to London.' Upon examination she was found guilty, 'and as a result (he) caused the poor old thing on a wintry market day in January to be set in the stocks very early in the morning. At nine o'clock, when the market was fullest of people, she was placed in a cart, with a paper set about her head on which was written "A reporter of false tales", and carried about the market place and other streets, tarrying wherever there was a crowd,' 'Young peoples and boyes of the town castyng snowballes at her.'

Then the aged woman was again set in the stocks and kept there till the market closed. Cromwell justified this punishment by saying, 'Thys was her penans; for I knewe no lawe otherwyse to punyshe her butt by discretion; trustyng itt shall be a warnyng to other lyght persons in such wyse to order their self. Howebeitt, I cannot perceyve but the seyd Image is not yett out of sum of ther heddes.'

The last two verses of an Elizabethan ballad entitled *A Lament for Walsingham* describe the situation well:

'Weepe, weepe, O Walsingham,
Whose dayes are nightes,
Blessings turned to blasphemies,
Holy deeds to dispites.

Sinne is where our Lady sate,
Heaven turned is to helle;
Satan sitte where our Lord did swaye,
Walsingham, oh, farewell!'

Happily Walsingham is once again robust. Although little of the original 'Nazareth' remains its spirit and intention thrive. The two original Holy Wells can be visited in the grounds of Walsingham Abbey. Once solely for religious use by the pilgrims, their water was reputed to cure the sick, especially those suffering from stomach disorders and headaches. Over the years they have degenerated into wishing wells, the wisher having to kneel upon a stone separating the wells, scooping out some water from each and making a silent and secret wish which the Virgin Mary is said to grant within a year so long as secrecy is maintained.

In 1931 it was decided by the Anglicans to build a replica of the original Holy House of Nazareth, but this time from brick replacing wood. When the foundations were excavated an ancient well was discovered which was thought to have been the site of the original Holy House. This well was incorporated in a wall of the new shrine. Over 100,000 pilgrims visit Walsingham each year and most are sprinkled at this holy well from which water is drawn in a long silver spoon. A little is used to make a cross on the pilgrim's forehead, some is sipped and the remainder is poured over the hands or any afflicted part of the body as the water is believed to have healing powers.

This Holy House is part of a large pilgrimage church. A replica of the statue of Our Lady was made at Chelsea where the original had been violated and burned. This is the focal point of the visit.

The beautiful little town has numerous shops selling a plethora of religious effigies and artefacts connected with a pilgrimage centre, all in varying degrees of taste. Clerical cloth brushes against leather and denim in the narrow pavements. All abilities are temporarily fused together, for holiness is everywhere in Little Walsingham.

The
Happisburgh
Smuggler

Today Happisburgh (pronounced 'Hazeboro') is a typical
North Norfolk coastal village, except that it has a fine
lighthouse built by Trinity House in 1791.

During the 18th century it was like so many of our coastal
communities, each with its band of smugglers running cargoes of
contraband goods from the continent. They were on occasion
aided by compliant coastguards and customs officials who were
willing to turn a blind eye for a suitable purse.

Despite the number of armed revenue officers patrolling our
shores and the preventative boats stationed at many seaside
villages, smuggling was a great source of corruption. People in
general considered the heavy import taxes which Sir Robert
Walpole's government had imposed on basic goods,
notwithstanding the luxurious type, to be iniquitous. Popular
sympathy was almost every time with the law breakers.

Numerous people from every walk of life shared in smuggled
goods, rather like the black market of the Second World War.
The fine lady yearned for her silk dresses, the housewife wanted
her cheap tea and lace, the squire his keg of brandy and French
wines, the farmer was pleased to fill his pipe with contraband
tobacco, and the parson sip his illegal gin.

Even the good Norfolk Parson Woodforde, diarist and vicar of
Weston Longeville from 1776–1803, wrote that he stayed up until
midnight on 17th May 1780 expecting, 'Richard Andrews the

honest smuggler with some gin.' On 2nd June 1788 he was 'Very busy this morning in bottling of two Tubs of Gin and one of Coniac (sic) Brandy ... which came in the night from (Moonshine) Buck from Honingham.'

Smuggling involved many vicious fights with the authorities, and gangs were lucky to get away with one cargo in three. At one time dragoons were quartered along the coast to deal with the escalating situation. In the churchyard at Old Hunstanton stands a gravestone erected to the memory of 'William Webb, late of the 15th D'ns [Dragoons] who was shot from his Horse by a party of Smugglers on the 26 day of Sepr 1784 Aged 26.'

Fighting and squabbling was also rife amongst the 'free-traders', which this strange tale will show.

One moonless night nearly 200 years ago there was the familiar silent roll of wagons filled with contraband heaving their way along the narrow coastal path, the smugglers well pleased with their night's work.

A small group of men were walking home shortly after the last cart had disappeared into the blackness. Their pleasure froze to horror when they witnessed a grotesque stranger coming up the main street from the direction of Cart Gap. This was no mortal being for although it moved at usual speed it was without legs. Its pigtailed head swung backwards between its shoulders. A pistol was thrust into its wide leather belt which fastened its sailor's uniform and a parcel was clutched close to its body.

Once the men had collected their wits some resolved to keep a future watch to see if the apparition returned. For several nights they waited in vain and then came success. The legless sailor floated up from the same direction with the parcel still in his arms, nothing was different except that his head was now the right way round. The watchers stalked their prey until it came to a deep well into which it dropped its parcel, which it followed without sound.

Their tale was not believed the following morning. The narrators were accused of having been on strong ale the night before, but in time their persistence paid off and the well was searched.

After much persuasion a volunteer made the frightening descent on a piece of rope firmly held by Happisburgh's strongest men. About 50 ft down his lantern showed a small piece of navy blue cloth caught on a projecting brick.

On his next journey he carried a long clothes prop so that he could probe the bottom of the well. The air was stiff with apprehensive excitement as the young man was pulled into daylight. His ashen face told all.

And so the brave lad made a third journey, this time armed with a large hook secured to a piece of rope which he painstakingly swung around the base of this loathsome well. He placed his eventual catch into a sack, which when opened revealed a pair of green rotting legs still wearing boots. The limbs had been hacked off at their thighs and the stench of putrid flesh sickened the onlookers.

The young man was told to go down for a fourth investigation but refused, in favour of a half-drunken fisherman who set off with an unfamiliar fishing line and hook. Much later he came up clutching a great mass of dripping cloth which he threw to the ground. It was the decomposed body of a man whose head had been severed except for a small thread at the back of his neck. He wore a sailor's uniform and had a pistol stuck into a wide leather belt.

A few weeks later evidence of the murder of a sailor came to light near Cart Gap. The twin pistol of that found in the dead man's belt was unearthed close to some gold coins and empty whisky bottles. Bloodstains were splashed on the ground. It was assumed there had been a quarrel between the 'freetraders', one had been killed and his head and legs hacked off to make it easier to conceal the body down the well, which had proved to be an uneasy resting place. The murderers were never discovered, neither was the identity of the Happisburgh Smuggler.

Bibliography

A Dyshe of Norfolk Dumplings
Walton N. Drew
Jarrold & Sons

Norfolk Portraits
R. W. Ketton-Cremer
Faber & Faber

Norfolk
Bernard E. Dorman
Batsford

*Royal Illustrated History of Eastern England
Vols I and II*
A. D. Bayne
James McDonald & Co., Great Yarmouth

East Anglian Coast and Waterways
Robert Simper
East Anglian Magazine Ltd.

Walsingham in Times Past
Rev Peter Rollings S.M.
Countryside Publication

The Companion Guide to East Anglia
John Seymour
Collins

*Victoria History of the County of Norfolk
Vol II*

Ballads, Songs and Rhymes of East Anglia
A. S. Harvey
Jarrold & Sons Ltd.

BIBLIOGRAPHY

East Anglia Magazine

English Country Life in the 18th Century
R. Bayne-Powell
John Murray

Ghosts and Witches
J. Wentworth Day
Batsford

The Prostitutes' Padre, The Notorious Rector of Stiffkey
Tom Cullen
Bodley Head

Poppy Land — Papers Descriptive of Scenery on the East Coast
Clement Scott
Jarrold & Sons

Poppyland — Strands of Norfolk History
Peter Stibbons and David Cleveland
Poppyland Publishing

Poppyland in Pictures
Elizabeth Jones
Poppyland Publishing

The Land of the Broads
E. R. Suffling
L. Upcott Gill

The Norfolk Garland
John Glyde, Jun.
Jarrold & Sons

Ghosts of the Broads
Chas. Sampson
Jarrold Colour Publications, Norwich

English Home-Life 1500–1800
Christina Hole
Batsford

Norfolk — A Changing Countryside
Susanna Wade Martins
Richard Clay Ltd.

Tales of Norfolk
Ida Fenn
Geo. K. Reeve Ltd.

Wetlands
David Bellamy and Brenda Quayle
Sidgwick & Jackson

The Burston School Strike
Bertram Edwards
Lawrence & Wishart, London

Admiral Lord Nelson
A. A. C. Hedges F.L.A.
Jarrold Colour Publications: Norwich

The Vocabulary of East Anglia
Robert Forby
David & Charles Reprints

More Murders in East Anglia
Robert Church
Robert Hale, London

History of Norfolk
Raymond Rye
Elliot Stock

Out of Norfolk
Seamen and Travellers
Peter Elphick
Orlando Publishing